LETTERS TO LUCY

LETTERS TO LUCY

LIVING BELOW SEE LEVEL

BY KATHY LONGTIN

XULON PRESS

Xulon Press
2301 Lucien Way #415
Maitland, FL 32751
407.339.4217
www.xulonpress.com

Unless otherwise indicated, Scripture quotations taken from the Holy Bible, New International Version (NIV). Copyright © 1973, 1978, 1984, 2011 by Biblica, Inc.™. Used by permission. All rights reserved.

Printed in the United States of America.

ISBN-13: 978-1-63221-465-2

Dedicated to my husband, Keith, aka "Napa,"
whose patient, forgiving love has always
overlooked my flaws to see our potential.

ACKNOWLEDGEMENTS

THIS BOOK WOULD NOT BE A REALITY WITHOUT THE encouragement of Patsy Clairmont, to whom I also owe the title and subtitle. I learned much from the four mentoring sessions I so enjoyed with her.

Thank you to Carol Darling and Michelle O'Neal, who read the manuscript and provided helpful feedback. Thanks also to Melanie Perschka, who let me bounce off ideas and provided support throughout. It was Melanie who signed up for Patsy Clairmont's mentoring sessions and made me envious enough to do the same.

Thanks to my kids, Jake and Renée, for their encouragement, and to Lucy and Lukas for being the greatest grandkids on the planet and the ones who inspired me to write about my adventures with God.

Thank you to Keith, who had to listen to all my ramblings and to every revision of every chapter. He did it with eagerness, even when I interrupted his shows!

I owe all thanks to God and to those who, in any way, have enriched my walk with Him.

TABLE OF CONTENTS

INTRODUCTION

LUCY?! THEY'RE NAMING HER LUCY?! OUR MINDS immediately went to the iconic sitcom character of the fifties—a scatter-brained redhead whose antics always caused havoc for her friends and long-suffering husband, Ricky. How could your parents scar our first grandchild like that?! We had visions of you being mercilessly teased by those who had cool twenty-first-century names—like Jennifer or Caitlyn... We saw bullies calling out, "Luuuuucy, I'm ho-me," a la Ricky, every time you passed on the playground. But never ones to interfere with our children's parenting decisions, (ah-hem), we gave them the benefit of the doubt. Said benefit evaporated when your father, ever the character himself, used his "Ricky" voice to show us how fun it was to use that very line when he came home from work. Sigh. Maybe we could come up with a nickname for you that would stick—uh, Lucinda? No, too Cruella de Ville. Lucia? A little operatic. Lucy in the Sky with Diamonds?... definitely not. As we ran out of options, your mother shed some light on the subject.

Yes, light. That's what your name means—Lucy means "Light"! In fact, "Lucy" in your parents' generation was more commonly recognized as the lead character of C. S. Lewis' *The Chronicles of Narnia*.[1] I love C. S. Lewis. Your name was becoming more acceptable and, more importantly, worthy of our first grandchild! You were certainly going to be the light in your parents' eyes and in ours. (I have to note here that your brother, Lukas, is just as bright a light in our lives, but my thoughts are those of a girl, so they might resonate more with you. Lukas, this is as much for you as for Lucy, and my life and thoughts are as open to you, but to publicly address all this "girl talk" directly to you might be seen as a threat to your man-card.)

Lucy, we now love your name, and we couldn't think of any other more appropriate for one who reflects God's light, even from a young age. It's God's light, ultimately, that is the subject of this book—His light in my life. I want to share it because there's a mass effort to snuff out His light these days. Some places have grown so dark, His light is hard to find. I'm not one to stand on a street corner with a megaphone or even be bold on Facebook. I don't even preach to you when we're spending time together—so you may miss it. You may not see the fire that drives me—and it's important to me—that whatever your life's choices, you understand how that fire worked in my life.

Jeremiah 20:9 says, "But if I say I will not mention his word or speak anymore in his name, his word is in my heart like a fire, a fire shut up in my bones. I am weary of holding it in. Indeed, I cannot." That was the foundational verse for VERVE, the drama ministry that I served with and learned so much from. VERVE means passion; fire. You have it. How will you use it? I can't wait to see. But for now, I invite you into The Chronicles of Nama.

I HAD IT ALL UNTIL THEY TOLD ME I DIDN'T

IN 1977, YOUR NAPA AND I WERE IN A GOOD SPACE— space #5 in La Palma Mobile Estates, San Diego, to be exact. We were homeowners for the first time, with two kids and a dog. We'd lived in trailers before, but this one earned the mobile home designation. It had a kitchen bay window and a pop-out living room. And, per our community's designation, we enjoyed the status of living on an "estate." At twenty-three, we'd realized the American dream.

Napa had earned this middle-class to riches story, but at the beginning, he hadn't earned his "Napa" title yet, so I knew him as "Keith." We met in high school and started dating when my boyfriend's car was out of commission for just long enough. Keith drove us home from school. At first, he'd drive me across town and then drop off my boyfriend. After a few days, he'd drop off my boyfriend and then drive me across town. I think it the highest compliment that he stooped to such devious manipulation for me! His scheme worked. We graduated together and dropped out of college together. He joined the navy in 1972, and added me to his seabag on September 8, 1973. That's when we left our parents' middle-class homes in St. Paul, MN, and towed all WE owned to Port Deposit, MD. There, he learned all about nuclear power, and I learned how to stretch Kool-aid into meals for the last days of a pay period. After six months there, we transferred to upstate New York. There, Keith got hands-on reactor training, and I got pregnant. That pregnancy didn't start well, so I miscarried soon into it. I was pregnant again when we left New York after ten months to drive cross-country to Keith's next duty station in San Diego. He was assigned to the USS Dixon, a submarine tender—sort of a "mother ship" for submarines. After just a few months there, he was transferred to his first submarine, the USS Pintado, also home-ported in San Diego. Keith received his first son and his first sub at about the same time in August 1975. The sub was cigar-shaped, so maybe celebratory for the birth of your Uncle Jacob? The party didn't last long. Just days later—and without my postpartum permission, the sub sailed to Bremerton, WA, for an overhaul. That was a year-long gig, so we hauled ourselves up there too. After the shipyards, we all returned to San Diego, and that's where our happy story continues.

As she hopes you remember, your mom was born in January, 1977, so she's just about sixteen months younger than Jacob. "Jake" was mellow and a schedule-keeper—an easy baby. Your mom was... not. But, with the same springy curls, sparking blue eyes, and innocent smile as her brother, she got away with a lot. As with Napa, she hadn't earned the title of "mom" yet, so we knew her as "Renée."

We were very proud of both our kids and proud to be part of the submarine community. Pintado even held the honor of having tested the DSRV—Deep Submergence Rescue Vehicle—and Keith was one of those who transferred to it twice, in DEEP water.

I have fond memories of visiting Keith on Pintado, or "the boat," as we knew it, when he had duty. We'd get to the pier after three ID checks, walk across the gangway to the top of the sub, have the "topside watch" radio down to tell "Petty Officer Longtin" we were there, and then it was into the hatch and down the ladder. Keith would take time to eat with us and show us around a little. I had no idea what I was looking at, but I felt proud that he did. I never got to see the reactor compartment where he and the other "nucs" worked—totally classified. Just before Jake was born, Pintado took family members out for a day on a "dependents' cruise." They demonstrated "angles and dangles" that they do to maneuver away from something quickly. This coincided with our lunch shift, so it had the feel of a restaurant on a roller coaster. When they fired a torpedo, we felt the boat jerk, our ears pop, and we heard the loud "whoosh" of its launch. Well, ok—for us, they just flooded the torpedo tube with pressurized water; we didn't get to blow anything up. It was still an experience well worthy of bragging rights.

Of course, unique jobs come with unique challenges. The thing about being married to a submariner is that his workplace might move after you drop him off in the morning. A "fast-attack" submarine, as Pintado was, is like a college kid away from home—unpredictable schedule, sometimes gone for months at a time, and only surfaces when she needs something. Family commitments came with caveats. The only things we could say with relative confidence were: 1) Pintado would be going out on Westpac in August and 2) we'd be transferred overseas early in 1978. A Westpac, for you civilians, is a Western Pacific cruise lasting six months or so—with no deck, verandas, portholes, or buffets. A fast attack's job is to locate and track enemy submarines. With Keith at sea so often, my mission was to locate and track inquisitive toddlers. It was all part of being a navy wife, and I was proud of that too.

I had all I wanted, until somebody told me I didn't. The women's movement geared up for a National Women's Conference that year, and I heard mixed messages. "As a woman, you can have it all and do it all! You don't have to be 'just a housewife'!" The language sounded inspiring and empowering, but challenging. I questioned my worth. I was Keith's wife, Jake and Renée's mom, but who was I, without those labels? I couldn't think of anything. I'd been a nurse's aide before marriage, but now? Their image of a successful woman looked like Barbie in a business suit, with matching heels and perfectly-coifed hair. My mirror showed a plain Jane—brown hair pulled back, no makeup, and puréed food stains on t-shirt and shorts. Oh Lucy, how I wish I'd been able to see that image as the working uniform of a mom whose heart was made up to fully engage. Our Enemy is so skilled at using inspiring-sounding popular messages to create dissatisfaction—and I took the bait. Over time, I swallowed the lie that I lacked identity and value as a stay-at-home mom. I regret to say that I stopped nursing Renée after just three months and went to work as a nurse's aide in a nursing home.

With my reflection professionalized in a crisp, white uniform, I left the messy chins and bottoms at home to clean those of geriatric strangers. One day, I picked up my paycheck with kids in tow. A nurse questioned me with shock and accusation: "You have two kids that young, and you're trying to work?!" I felt the truth of her words, but I held a paycheck with MY name on it. Fortunately, I had to quit that job soon after, when the babysitter I'd hired through the want ads proved unreliable.

Lucy, I love that you know so many Christian songs and artists—do you remember Elevation Worship's song, "See a Victory"[2]? One line says, "You take what the enemy meant for evil, and you turn it for good..." Spoiler alert: God had a plan.

For some incomprehensible reason, I couldn't find another employer that would hire a temporarily single mom with two kids under two who would be moving in six months. Where could I find a nametag worthy of respect? I tried to volunteer. Nothing. I couldn't even work for the Red Cross without attending an orientation that I couldn't attend.

If I couldn't volunteer in the community, I'd volunteer at church. They never turn anybody down. Keith doesn't remember that Presbyterian church, but I was an occasional pew-warmer. Both of us had been raised in church—I even sang in the choir and in a gospel musical. But once married, we marginalized God until we had kids. Then it seemed good to "teach them about God." God's pilot light still burned in us; we just hadn't turned up the flame. The light wasn't bright enough yet for me to see who I was.

I signed up to teach Sunday school—two-year-olds. Then I found out they actually had lesson plans for that age—it wasn't just a babysitting gig. That was more than I'd bargained for, but I'd committed. As I prepared to teach, I re-engaged with God's Word. Keith prepared for Westpac. I wrote him the first letter the week before the boat left: "...[God's reach] extends far below the surface of the Pacific too. God can be a tremendous support, if you let Him. Take Him for real, at least in practice for a while. When you get really mad or depressed, let Him help shoulder the burden...when something goes right, let Him know that too. Most important, let Him love you."

I meant it. I was confident. That week.

"How can a young person stay on the path of purity?
By living according to your Word." Psalm 119:9

Chapter Two

ANGLES AND DANGLES

THIS MONTHS-LONG SEPARATION THING WAS NEW TO us, and my new confidence started doing its own "angles and dangles" right off the bat. Nary a week after I wrote that encouraging letter, I wrote:

> ...my head is spinning. I feel like I'm in shock. I'll bet you feel the same way sometimes. I'm scared to death—I can't get Xmas presents started 'til I'm sure I'm financially secure. I'm scared I won't be able to sell the bike (Keith's motorcycle he left me to sell)—I'm scared somebody may rip it off. ...I'm so confused. With all of my friends and supports, nobody can give me the support I'm used to receiving from you. Help! Right now, I'm not sure I want to go to church tomorrow or volunteer for anything. I'd like to go to bed and stay there

for a week, at least. Renée's crying—driving me up the WALL!

If *America's Got Talent* had a category for saying the wrong thing at the wrong time, I could win. Keith lived in a metal tube that could sink or explode at any moment. He dealt with the anxiety of keeping up with the boat's demands, its strict schedule, didn't get enough sleep, missed us terribly—and he got a "HELP!" letter from me. Fortunately, I didn't write too many like that. Thank God for grace.

Keith found some solace in music and cards. His love of bridge was born on that cruise. (That love dealt him in with a pack of zippy and zany seniors some thirty years later.) His best times, though, were when the boat pulled into port—Japan, South Korea, the Philippines, Guam. He wrote the most about Hong Kong. He called it a "tourist's paradise" in contrast to the liberty ports with the "Buy me drinkie?" girls. I loved that he loved to sightsee and didn't take some liberties that others did. I've always had reason to trust him.

Three weeks into the Westpac, I found out through navy channels that we'd be transferred next to Sardinia, Italy, in about three to four months. You may have to look that up on a map—I did too. Keith had no such communication. I wrote him of it the same day I found out, but mail doesn't do well at keeping up with submarines. By the time he got that letter, it was one of thirty-five I'd written. I wrote long letters of vital current events: Jake sneezed out boogers, I had to rip out too much of a crochet project, I shouldn't have had mac and cheese for lunch, Sam's gonna kill Marlena on *Days of*

Our Lives... As Keith described later, he tore through them, asking, "Where the [*bleep*] are we going?!"

I had to prepare for the move to Italy while Keith was out to sea. Our sponsor wrote us a letter both helpful and intimidating. A sponsor is a sailor who's about to transfer back from the duty station you're going to and so can offer advice and assistance. I had to obtain passports, shots, warmer clothes, large rugs, kitchen cabinets, and transformers and then prepare a household-goods shipment, an express shipment, a shipment to store in MN, arrange to have the car shipped to Italy, prepare it for shipment, and then drive it to the port it would ship from. Finally, I needed to sell the mobile home.

Have you ever heard the expression, "They also serve who only stand and wait?[3]" It's an old quote more recently applied to military families whose service members are deployed. As much as we military families appreciate our support being recognized as service to the country, ask a military spouse if she only "stands and waits." I'll be right behind you—at a safe distance.

Teaching Sunday school became one too many things, so I went back to being a spectator Christian. One Sunday, the church hosted a guest missionary who spoke. He truly inspired me and my feelings overflowed in a letter to Keith. I described the man's life in Nepal and added, "I wonder how an 'older man' [in his fifties or sixties] could leave the comfortable life of this country for the physical and political dangers of Nepal?" I stated that the answer was obvious—"that's what Christianity is all about! Makes you think, doesn't it? My problems all melted down to nothing, just listening to him talk. This confirms my conviction to raise the kids knowing God, because God's where it's at. I want church to be the

center of our lives and our closest friends to be those from church."
I felt re-charged. One letter, from late September, best shows how
I was dealing with everything three weeks after that one. Our car
was in the shop with transmission problems, and I was waiting to
hear back about it. I wrote Keith:

> Why do I have this gut feeling they'll be keeping
> the car overnight? Why aren't you here? Somehow,
> even while writing that question, I know the
> answer. God is letting me know that when I have
> to, I can take care of myself. I get the feeling that
> He already knows this to be true. Yesterday, in my
> letter, I started to tell you how secure I felt about
> the future. As you can see from my letters, I have
> my definite highs and lows. Through it all, I never
> doubted for a moment that both of us would make
> it through Westpac and be a lot stronger for it. That
> strength doesn't come from me—I just don't have
> it. I no longer have any doubt that there exists an
> extremely powerful force that's not only keeping
> me from falling apart, but giving me an excitement
> about the rest of my life. Now that my belief in
> God is firmly rooted, the pieces of my life are begin-
> ning to fit together. I know now that my interest
> in medicine was necessary to give me a feeling of
> self-importance. Now I feel I can break that tie
> and follow the real interests that are uniquely my
> own—crocheting, knitting, and macramé. The
> more thought I give it, the more excited I get about

my yarn shop. I'd like to embark on that project independently...with the double standard the way it is, if we entered a joint business venture, my name would be totally ignored.

In summing up, my goals are 1) to strengthen our marriage and to shift interest to "you" instead of "me"; 2) to keep a close relationship with the kids and raise them knowing God; 3) to learn everything there is to know about crocheting and become a master of that; 4) to become as knowledgeable as time permits of knitting, macramé, and all things related to yarn; 5) to learn guitar and piano well enough to fake it. All of this is with the assumption that everything I do will be to serve God and He will be the center of our (I hope) lives. End of sermon. The point of this whole thing was to tell you that I miss you terribly, but I've got my act together and I look forward to your return with new vigor.

Hmmm...looking back on that, I like where I was at that moment—had some tweaking to do, but that would come.

Have you ever noticed how quickly resolve can morph into rationalization and then self-pity? My strength often looked porous. One Sunday, I wrote Keith:

"Church really got to me today. I haven't been to a church service yet since you left that I didn't shed a tear during part of it. The service itself was very uplifting. Everything was going swell until the end. They sang 'Pass It On'—a song about spreading God's love. There were two couples—one on either side of me—and they both put their arms around each other. That was all I needed—I hung tough through the benediction, but then I grabbed the kids and left."

One Sunday, a very kind lady found me crying, listened to my story, and invited me to sit with her. I did—once. In my last weeks before I went home to MN, it was easier to take the less emotional route and escape to Fiesta Island. The island was an actual garbage dump in the middle, but on its pristine outer edge, you could dump your cares into the scenic Mission Bay. I'd grab the Sunday paper, pile the kids and dog in the car, drive through McDonald's for a pancake breakfast, and plop us all down in the sand to watch sailboats for a while. I found it less lonely to be alone than to be a single surrounded by couples.

I made a point to encourage Keith in every letter, but one day, overwhelming emotions spilled out to form my worst letter:

"Dear Keith, I want a divorce. I think I can grow more fully on my own—even with the kids and Daffy. Their lives revolve around me, but right now my life revolves around you, and that's wrong. I'm not a person in my own right, just attached by various labels to you...YOU get orders for Italy. I worry, plan, fight my way through navy channels to get your kids and household goods over there... The mobile home may not be sold for quite a few more months.

Who goes to Italy? NOT ME!! Somebody has to stay in the states to finalize the sale...you can pay lip service to the business about the mobile home, but come Feb. 15th and it's not sold, who will be where, doing what about it?!" I ended the letter with "I love you. PS. Of course I don't want a divorce, but we need to talk when you get home."

I never mailed the letter; I wouldn't have. Keith never saw it until recently. We'd agreed that the "D" word wouldn't be uttered in our marriage. I kept the letter because it recorded my struggle for identity. My letters to Keith served as my diary. I look back now and thank God that my life "revolved around Keith's"—greatest blessing of my life.

On most days, I didn't have time for an identity crisis, anyway. The "to-do" list had to be completed by drop-dead dates. Most of my letters describe that progress. I did manage to get everything done for the transfer, except for selling the mobile home. I left that with the realtor and went home to Minnesota in mid-November, to wait for Keith.

In December, Keith had a little excitement he'd not soon forget. Here's the Wikipedia version: "Following her year of routine training, Pintado deployed to the Western Pacific in August 1977. She was operating with Republic of Korea navy vessels on 6 December 1977 when a South Korean surface ship abruptly turned towards her. She executed a crash dive, but the two ships collided, and Pintado sustained damage to the top of her rudder."[4]

Keith's version was a bit more subjective: "I sure am glad I'm able to write this, really. On Dec. 6th, we were hit by a S. Korean destroyer. When the word was passed, 'Collision Imminent,' I sat down and prepared to kiss my ass goodbye. He just hit the top of the rudder and smashed it up. We were very lucky. I'll tell you more about that incident when I get home." At home, he described the tense moments after they felt the jolt of the impact. "Was that it? Was it over?" Everybody held their breath as damage control reports from all stations fired in to confirm they were still intact.

He also told me that the "Collision Imminent" word was passed again the very next day, but a collision was narrowly avoided and the offender was a small fishing vessel that would have lost that match-up.

Keith transferred off Pintado in Guam and flew to San Diego. He celebrated New Year's Eve twice, as he crossed the international date line. To add to our celebration, he signed the papers for the sale of the mobile home while in San Diego. Then he flew into my very grateful arms in Minnesota. It was him and his seabag full of smelly laundry—submarine smell, a submariner's wife's favorite. It meant our guys were home.

I'd been in St. Paul with our parents for a month and a half. With Keith, we were there for another few weeks. It can be a little tense when you go back home as adult children, but grandkids have a way of commanding attention away from any tension, so it was a re-generating time. Our nuclear family was back together again, and that was the main source of our comfort. It was just in time for God to pull us out of our comfort zones again, to resolve that decade's identity crisis.

"May my cry come before you, LORD; give
me understanding according to your word."
Psalm 119:169

CHAPTER THREE

BUILDING ON LA ROCCIA, THE ROCK

LUCY, DO YOU REMEMBER WHEN WE MADE "FLAT LUKAS" and "Flat Lucy" to take you along with us on our European River Cruise? Those flat grandkids became so real to us that, during a photoshoot of you in our cabin, I panicked when "you" slipped into a teeny crevice between the bed and closet! The ship's staff feigned compassion but didn't respond to the emergency with a saw or crowbar, so I had to come up with a plan or write a story about how you met such good friends on the inside of the ship that you couldn't possibly leave them. WE couldn't leave YOU, however, so after two days, I FINALLY finessed you out of there with sheets of paper. We were so relieved at your rescue, we texted your mom immediately with the reunited family photo. Napa and I wanted you with us so badly because we've always loved to travel and we wanted to share that love with you—even by proxy.

That said, travel feels more comfortable when I have a return ticket in hand, and we didn't when the day came for our transfer to Italy. The boarding call announcement said, "It's time to leave everything familiar to live in a strange land."

We clung to both sets of parents at the airport, inwardly screaming, "Don't let us go! Let's go back home!" But the preparations were complete, and Keith's orders were not suggestions. I thought of the poster in the recruiter's office—"The navy's not just a job; it's an adventure!" This was the 4D version.

The night before our flight, the clouds over NYC poured out their welcome—the worst blizzard the city had seen in over three decades. Our original flight was cancelled, and we telegrammed our sponsor that we'd be a day late. We knew that he planned to pick us up at the airport in Olbia, Sardinia. No cell phones, no internet yet—if you can imagine such a world. We arrived at JFK and made our way through icy puddles to a cab with the two bundled babies, their three toys, a diaper bag, and a crated dog—to the TWA terminal. We waited in line to learn that our replacement flight was also cancelled. I wrote my parents later: "At 6:55 p.m., Keith told me we were taking a Pan Am flight leaving at 8:00. Since Pan Am was in another terminal, I turned to tell him he was nuts when he picked up Daffy's crate and headed out the door. What could I do? I grabbed both kids, the diaper bag, Punkinhead, Bunny Ball, and Humpty and followed him through more snowy puddles, into another cab." We caught that 8:00 flight, but our luggage didn't. It would catch up in about a week.

Our first view of Italy—soldiers armed with machine guns on the tarmac. We exhaled when we found out they weren't looking for us. In Rome, we'd booked a room at the Holiday Inn for the thirteen-hour layover, to free the dog from her prison. Good thing. Renée'd had diarrhea all the way over, using up the diapers in my bag. I sent Keith down to ask about disposable diapers. They sent up an overgrown Kotex pad that—I would later learn—would fit into an Italian pants thing which I didn't have. So, I "borrowed" a towel for the trip to Olbia. I kept that for about thirty years, just in case they tracked me down and wanted it back. On the plane to Olbia, a large dog had its own seat. The flight attendants handed out liquor-filled candy—probably to put us into a stupor as our pilot dive-bombed into the black night. We hoped he saw something we didn't. We made it to Olbia, but our sponsor didn't. He didn't get the telegram until too late, so he had driven down the night before. Two American guys were waiting for other new Americans who hadn't made our flight. They took us to Palau, our final destination. In their back seat, we wondered why he was taking back roads. He laughed. "These are the main roads. Welcome to Italy."

It was then late at night, but he stopped at an American's house to get Pampers for us, and then we met our sponsor at "La Roccia Hotel." La Roccia means "the rock." The hotel was actually built around a HUGE rock. We would be anchored to it for a couple of months while we awaited housing and our shipments from the states. I was the only washing machine and our balcony served as dryer, but Segnore Marcos, the very kind owner, provided the kitchen facilities for navy families' use during off hours.

I woke up the first morning wondering if it had all been a nightmare. The sea of red-tiled roofs visible from our balcony dashed that hope. First thing—how to find food. God provided two Christian navy families in the hotel for help. We could buy fruit and vegetables at the local Italian markets, but our commissary and exchange were on another island, Santo Stefano. It wasn't like hopping in a car and driving to your Giant Eagle. No bridge. We walked to the Palau pier and waited for the navy's gray liberty boat. It was covered and held maybe fifty people. The two sailors tied up to the pier and then loaded us all on board. In calm weather, it was just a half-foot up maybe. In rougher seas, you kind of tossed the kids up, one at a time, and hoped the sailors could catch. Free of them, you handed up your shopping cart and timed your jump. It was more interesting coming back, when the cart was full of groceries.

Keith's new workplace was moored at Santo Stefano. He was assigned to the USS Howard Gilmore—a submarine tender. Keith's division tended to the radiological needs of visiting subs. He didn't warm up to the Gilmore right away. It wasn't the "family" atmosphere of the submarine, and the "nucs" were thought cliquish and arrogant (no comment, I was a nuc's wife and proud of it!).

Keith had more free time early on, so we'd walk to get our bearings. I wrote mom and dad that we loved the land—the deep blue Mediterranean, the rugged cliffs—and the food, including pizza (with prosciutto), calzone, calamari, cappuccino, and fresh panini. The shrimp stared back at you from the plate, but once you cut off the eyes and moved them out of sight, you'd enjoy the freshest shrimp ever. As soon as we had the car, we explored northeastern Sardinia—Costa Smeralda, the "Emerald Coast." One of the highlights was a cork processing plant and gift shop in Tempio. Did you know that cork is the bark of a cork tree? We passed many cork trees on the way up. Cork in the raw is rough, like the bark of other trees—not the smooth, processed corkboard that we know. Once at the shop, we worked through hand signals and my few Italian words to have a conversation with the owners. All of us appreciated the others' efforts toward this human connection. When Mrs. Owner waved as we drove away, we felt the thrill of victory in our cross-cultural exchange. If I were more cynical, I might say that Mrs. Owner felt the thrill of our cash in her till, after we bought a mug set, two pieces of artwork, and a cork journal.

Of course, there were those clumsier interactions. One morning, the kids and I ventured out on our own to the local bakery for fresh panini. A short, elderly woman dressed entirely in black approached us and snatched Renée out of my arm. My American instinct was to scream and grab her back, but I figured I could take the old lady if she tried anything. She just wanted to love on "la bambina." We'd get used to that.

On another occasion, I'd maneuvered the stroller through a crowded flea market just to reach the top of some steps I couldn't get around. With Jake holding my other hand, I started to ease the stroller with Renée on board, down the steps. The noisy marketplace came to a standstill, with cries of "O bambini!" An Italian woman grabbed the front of the stroller, and we eased it down to the bottom. After a few curious stares, the market returned to chaos.

We Americans who lived there were mostly well-liked—after all, we were a huge boon to their economy. A few said they considered us more "residents" than the Italian tourists who tripled the population in the summer. One group who did NOT like our presence was the Communist Red Brigades, who would come through town every so often to make that known. These were the terrorists who kidnapped, imprisoned, and finally assassinated Aldo Moro—former Italian prime minister and leader of the Christian Democratic Party.

Shore patrol would pass the word any time the Red Brigades were expected, and we'd all lay low until they left. Not long before we arrived, they'd bombed five American cars. On one of our trips through Europe, we'd finally found a campground for the night when we saw red flags featuring a hammer and sickle at the entrance. We quickly did an about face and headed our Mazda station wagon with its US Armed Forces plates to a hotel across town.

After two months in "La Roccia," we started to settle in— -to daily life and, finally, to our new home—the bottom half of a duplex, in the small town of Porto Pozzo, about nine miles away from Palau. The gray cement structure had no central heat and no insulation, but it had a clothesline in the back. I had two kids in cloth diapers and no dryer. Drinking water came from a central well in a town several miles away, up on the mountain. The only kitchen cabinets or countertop were the three free-standing ones that I had bought in the states. I burned up the vacuum cleaner by plugging its cord into the wrong voltage outlet on the transformer. We had roaches the size of those in Florida, and spraying was futile. There were no stores in Porto Pozzo. We could drive to Palau, but if it was afternoon, the stores were closed—SIESTA. They might open later; they might not. Trips to the commissary or exchange were only by liberty boat, so they had to be planned ahead. All of the navy services and many of our friends were on yet another island, La Maddalena ("La Madd") and four Italian ferries served that route. You drove your car on board, and then it was forty minutes to get there from the Palau pier. If you wanted to get together with friends in another town or island, you planned ahead. If you couldn't make it, there was no way to tell them. We had no TV or telephone—for two years.

We loved it. Life was hard, and we'd been stripped of everything we thought we had control over. Americans were the minority there and had to adapt to the Sardinians' way of life. Those who couldn't adapt, didn't. They complained incessantly and escaped to the states whenever possible. I wrote mom and dad: "Both of us feel that people who say they don't like it here are denying the existence of culture shock, instead of allowing themselves to go through it and adjust."

We took two vacations to explore Europe during our two-year stay—once with the kids, once without. We camped through northern Italy, Germany, Denmark, Switzerland, and the Netherlands. We toured Anne Frank's house, visited all of Ludwig's castles, rode a cable car to the top of the Zugspitze, saw Hans Christian Andersen's home, enjoyed Munich's Oktoberfest and the original Legoland in Denmark. We waited forever for Renée to finish an ice cream cone at Tivoli Gardens (it was very rich) and then negotiated her temper tantrum at The Little Mermaid statue in Copenhagen. With the ship, Keith visited Yugoslavia; Barcelona and Majorca in Spain; Andorra and Toulon, France. En route to a conference, I stumbled on a Pope-led mass at the Vatican, visited Mozart's home and grave, and saw sites from *The Sound of Music* in Austria. Closer to "home," we toured caverns of Sardinia and took the ferry to explore the cliffs of Corsica. As we walked through history, we were challenged, informed, humbled...and we grew together as we tackled the adventure of getting around.

Before the first of those trips, the adventure of daily life became more routine. I stood at our open window, looked at the deep blue Med, and wrote mom and dad: "It's so nice to be able to have complete control of my days without TV, phones, or other demands on me. When Keith comes home, we enjoy each other and the kids totally since we are the other's entertainment. Our marriage is probably at its peak right now." Lucy, we still often look back to those days and remember how life-changing they were in their simplicity. We treasure that forced time out of our hectic, distracted, selfish, normal routine.

We did have Armed Forces radio and a stereo to play albums on [Google it]. We had two portable heaters, an electric blanket, and lots of warm clothes. When it rained, I put a portable heater in the bathroom with the diapers on a portable clothes line overnight. To live with roaches, we stomped our feet as we got out of bed to make them scatter, then rinsed the handful in the tub down the drain. We didn't only manage; we thrived.

We made good friends and networks among the Americans. I joined the wives club right away as I always had. My upstairs neighbor was past president of it and nominated me for "chaplain" of the group. It just meant I opened meetings with prayer, sent out greeting cards for life events, and helped with bazaars and such. Some women asked me to teach them how to crochet, so I started a class for seven women. I joined the local chapter of "Women of the Chapel" (WOC), an organization of protestant American military wives stationed in Europe.

It was through Bible studies with the WOC that I realized what a mindless downgrade it was to equate my identity or value to a subculture's definition of personal achievement. My childhood knowledge of "Jesus Loves Me" grew. That God-confidence ushered in self-respect, respect for Keith, and the knowledge that supporting my family was the most worthwhile thing I could be doing. With two kids under three, the needed support at the time was managing the home front. One day, I wrote home: "Thank God for no television—let somebody else try to live up to those ridiculous images."

God started our Italian life in La Roccia Hotel and helped us rebuild our lives on Him—THE ROCK.

"Your decrees are the theme of my song,
wherever I lodge." Psalm 119:54

Chapter Four

JUST CALL ME CHRISTIAN

IN FEBRUARY OF 1979, FOUR OF US FROM THE LOCAL
WOC attended a central event in Berchtesgaden, Germany, with
military wives stationed all over Europe.

The conference itself expanded on the women's studies we'd
enjoyed in the local chapter. I wrote my parents: "We gained prac-
tical knowledge on how to see our family as our mission field and
live as witnesses, while in training for an intimate relationship with
God." At the end of the conference, there was an optional session
on speaking in tongues. I wasn't sure what that was all about, but
two girls in my company claimed this gift and so we went. I was
intrigued enough to buy the speaker's "how-to" book.

We didn't have much opportunity to talk on the crowded
return train. Three of us were crammed in one side of our car with
three German men crammed in the other, our knees retracted to
keep from touching. I'd picked up a cold and was making rude
noises as I tried in vain to breathe through my nose. The German

guy opposite me offered me what looked like a styptic pencil. I politely shook my head, but he demonstrated its use by holding it to his nostril and offered it again. I hesitantly accepted and stuck it lightly up my nose. I jumped at the strong smell, setting the car to laughing, but I could breathe! I handed it back and thanked him profusely. Another meeting of two cultures without words—priceless.

At home, I read the book on gifts of the Spirit, prayed by my bedside as directed, and practiced speaking in tongues. What came out didn't sound like any foreign language or any gift, but I kept at it as long as I could while the kids napped. I tried very hard to convince myself that I'd succeeded because the book said that any doubt was of Satan. When Keith came home from work, he hadn't even closed the door when I announced, "I spoke in tongues!"

There have been a number of occasions in which Keith did not know what to make of me, and this was one of those. He ran to a fellow "nuc" on the ship, even though we were very involved with the protestant services and good friends with Chaplain Rubino. Keith knew Peter Keegan to be smart, wise, and often seen with a Bible in hand. When Peter learned that I'd been reading a book on Acts, he loaned us a tape series [Google it] on the book of Acts. It was from a seminary course—from the then-Sunset School of Preaching in Lubbock, Texas—now the Sunset Bible Institute. We had never studied the Bible like that before—with historical and cultural context, word studies going back to the original language for meaning, etc. For every question, Peter answered with a book, scripture references, or more tapes. This took months. I read the Bible at every opportunity and couldn't get enough. I'd read parts of it before, of course, but this was like my later addiction to Candy

Crush. It didn't read like fiction created by extremists—it read like an ancient newspaper—places, dates, people, and events that could be checked out. Finally, Peter came and spent the weekend with us. His wife, Susan, was at the Naval Hospital in Naples, having a baby. Our dispensary in La Madd wasn't equipped for deliveries, and husbands were not allowed to accompany their wives to Naples for lack of a place to put them. Since these things had to be planned ahead, most of those births were C-section. I think God worked out this weekend for Peter too, to keep his mind as distracted as possible. We occupied him with questions late into the night. Finally, we asked him about his church affiliation. "What do you mean you're not part of a denomination?! OK, yes Christian, but what brand?! What does your tag say?" Nope, just Christian. In all our twenty-five years, we'd not encountered non-denominationalism.

Through our studies, we came to believe that we needed to be immersed—baptized. (We'd been sprinkled as babies, but we'd not been consulted.) My other book on Acts had mentioned the same thing, so I'd talked to Chaplain Rubino about it. He was Baptist and was happy to baptize us—in the Mediterranean Sea. For him, baptism was "an outward sign of an inward grace." The whole church came, and we all celebrated. But then, after talking with Peter and further study with the tapes, we decided that we needed to be baptized again, this time with the belief that it was for the forgiveness of sins and the entry point into the life of grace. And so, just a month after Chaplain Rubino baptized us, Peter baptized Keith, and then Keith immersed me. You may have heard me joke that being baptized twice in the Mediterranean Sea merits extra credit in heaven?! Seriously, as I write this, I don't believe that the second dunking was necessary, but that's the date we told God, "We're all in." This memoir makes no claim to be a theological treatise, but that moment proved to be the most pivotal point in the direction of our faith associations. We saw ourselves as leaving denominational Christianity for first-century Christianity, and so we left our denominational fellowships to devour Bible studies with the Keegans' group. I left my post at Women of the Chapel—maybe unnecessarily, but we had to act on our beliefs at the time. I don't know where we'd be if we'd not made this change, but God has so poured out blessings on us through friends and opportunities to use our gifts that we can have no regrets.

I love God's sense of humor and timing, except maybe when the joke's on me. The very day after our second baptism, Keith and I were to be in charge of the protestant service. Chaplain Rubino had asked me to be his lay leader—to lead the service when the ship was out. The ship was out, but Keith had stayed in this time. There was no way to communicate with the chaplain, and he was counting on us. That Sunday morning, we did lead—I introduced Keith, and he delivered the sermon—on the importance of Bible study.

The navy community has no secrets, so before we had a chance to tell him, Chaplain Rubino found out we were baptized again. He was Sicilian, so his smile didn't mask his disappointment very well. We loved the chaplain and his wife, Sandra, but we'd made an important decision that led to the consequence of our serving God in separate ways.

There were seven of us at the Keegans' Italian apartment in La Madd. We did life together as often as living on separate islands could afford—at least weekly, and it'd be for most of the day, since it took so long to get there. We ate, gabbed, and studied the courses from the Sunset School. My favorite course from Sunset was Christian Historical Evidences—I did that on my own when Keith was at work or at sea. I had to constantly push the back button on the tape player to decipher it and keep up with notes. Until then, I had little idea of the overwhelming evidence supporting the Bible. These studies provided a solid foundation for my faith, which I would refer back to often.

While the Keegans bonded with their new baby, we and the other couple toured Venice and Florence together. St. Mark's square, pigeons, canal tour, hand-blown glass shop, freezing at the top of the Duomo in Florence, artwork overload, sleeping on the train...so grateful to have those memories to relive. Lucy, Napa and I hope you and Lukas will write your own such adventures for our great-great-grandchildren!

It always took effort to get together at the Keegans', but one night stands out in my memory. The ship was out to sea for ten days, and the kids and I were to visit with Sue and baby Miriam. We drove to the pier in Palau only to find the ferries on strike— only one of the four ferries to LaMadd was operating. Long lines of cars waited, and the ticket office was jammed with people pushing and yelling for tickets. The smart thing to do would have been to go back home, but no. I wedged my car in line, pushed and yelled my way through the office, and got a ticket. We had over an hour to wait in the car. Jake had to go potty. Nowhere to go. I told him to do the opposite of what I'd been training him to do for months. We finally reached Sue's place, I washed and hung Jake's pants on the line, and we enjoyed a short evening. We couldn't get home that night with the strike on, so Sue put the three of us in her extra bed. Sometime later, Renée fell out, slicing her upper eye lid. It needed stitches, but we weren't sure the dispensary was open and it would not at all be easy to get there. Sue had butterfly bandages, so we taped up the lid as best we could. In the morning, I got up before anyone else—we had to get in line for the early ferry—the only one I could count on to get us home that day. Jake's corduroy pants were still wet, so I borrowed a blanket and a chunk of bread and left Sue a note. I was never so grateful to catch a ferry. At home, our two dogs looked crazed and had trashed the place, but they were alive and very happy to see us.

I have so many other "Italy stories," but I'll burden you with just a few more. Orso, the dog Keith rescued from Santo Stefano, ran through our plate glass door. We drove thirty miles of winding, narrow roads to the Italian vet. He stitched her up. She ripped them out. I took her back, and this time, there was no anesthesia. I listened to her scream from the waiting room. She ripped them out again. We let her heal naturally.

Our landlady's adult son, about twenty, died tragically in a car accident, and the whole town walked by on the dirt road in front of our window, up the hill, to see his un-embalmed body lie in an open casket in their living room. We wimped out, closed our blinds, and didn't go, but deeply apologized later for that affront. At least at that time, they didn't embalm—you had to bury your loved one quickly.

One tragedy specifically grieved the navy community. As the ship pulled up anchor to set sail for ten days, the last mooring line snapped under tension and whiplashed back to the stern, catching the XO (executive officer) across his neck and upper chest. The ten-inch-diameter rope killed him instantly and injured three others who were with him.

After only a few months with the Keegans' group, it was time for us to make arrangements for our next duty station back in the states. The pile of tasks was even more daunting than for the transfer to Italy, but we and the Keegans left Sardinia about the same time, so the camaraderie helped ease the burden. Peter was getting out of the navy and would eventually work to help Three Mile Island clean up from their meltdown. Keith would be an instructor at the prototype in upstate NY where he'd been a student. But not yet. We were going to NY to find a house, but then he had months left in Italy and I would wait in MN with our families. As we made arrangements to transfer back, I wrote our parents that we'd miss Sardinia very much but were looking forward to meeting more of our church family in the states. Peter advised us that the institution of the "church of Christ" may look differently than our small family group had, but to be agents of change, if necessary. We were on fire, and we felt firmly-based in our knowledge of scripture and ready to change the world.

Oscar Wilde said, "The old believe everything; the middle-aged suspect everything; the young know everything."[5] We were young.

"How sweet are your words to my taste, sweeter than honey to my mouth!" Psalm 119:103

Chapter Five

REVERSE CULTURE SHOCK

LUCY, WITH ALL THE LOVE A NAMA CAN HAVE FOR A grandchild, I have to confess that your early notes on the viola were abrasively painful to hear. Yes, we applauded because we love you and appreciated your effort, but it took all that to keep our facial muscles from cringing at those scratchy notes. As you practiced and received more instruction, the sounds became melodic. When we could recognize the songwriter's message, we enjoyed listening.

Well, after our early efforts at deeper Bible study, God's song too often sounded scratchy to those I played to. I wanted everyone to hear of our new discoveries, fully expecting that they'd change their lives as we had. 1 Peter 3:15 says, "…always be prepared to give an answer to everyone who asks you to give the reason for the hope that is in you. But do it with gentleness and respect…" I may have missed that last part. I'm afraid God's message of love sounded more like my arrogance. In Italy, I was like the Psychology 101 student who carries a couch in his breast pocket. I jumped in to diagnose and treat all my friends' spiritual errors. At home in Minnesota, I felt compelled to retrain my mother. She'd had a faith relationship her whole life and was active in church for my whole life. I wrote Keith of my frustrations: "Our relationship is fine when we talk of shallow things, but when I bring up weightier matters, she doesn't want to talk." I wonder why.

When Keith returned from Italy, we set up our new life in New York and went into reverse culture shock, even though we'd never heard of such a thing. We felt enslaved to the clock that knew no siestas. Noise bombarded and interrupted from every direction—ringing telephones, doorbells, bustling traffic, TV with its incessant advertising demands. After briefly tuning in to our old TV set, we unplugged it for as long as we could. And you'd think we'd have loved the ease of finding food, but all those decisions! In Italy, we had a choice of three cereals, and you took the one that expired most recently. Here, we had more than five choices of just Cheerios! I had a professor once who said, "People in Russia drink because they don't have any choices; in the US, they drink because they have too many." I could relate. In Italy, shopping was a social event, with a relaxing boat ride on the Mediterranean before the drive home. In the states, it was a timed scavenger hunt with a do-or-die race to stand in line before the bumper-car race to the exit. To Jake and Renée, everything was brand new. Jake asked why people were driving into their houses; he'd never seen an attached garage. We could only wonder what else their little minds were trying to process. Jake could have started school then, but we decided to hold him back a year.

I have to brag on Keith—during this phase, he bought me a piano. I'd grown up trying to play. My family moved from

Minneapolis to St. Paul when I was seven, and the house came with a downright ugly upright in the basement. My parents didn't want to give me lessons to play THAT, so my friend Julie took lessons and then taught me. Dad just closed the door to the basement when I played. Keith didn't have a door to close—the piano he gave me was in our living room. He bore my practice sessions with the same teeth-gritting love that we showed for your early viola practice. For me, his pain was worth it—it soothed my soul. We had that piano until we moved into our current condo. I wish I still had it, but I hadn't played often—either too busy or it would make the dogs howl. I also wish I could have known my grandmother on my dad's side—she taught piano lessons. I have her name—Kathleen; I'd just like her talent.

As soon as we'd arrived in NY, we found a church in Clifton Park, about half an hour away from our house in Saratoga Springs. We threw ourselves in. We went Sunday mornings, Sunday evenings, and Wednesday nights. Beyond that, we attended a one-on-one "New Christians Class." We didn't see ourselves as "new Christians," but the preacher did, and his grandfatherly attention captivated us. And, we helped clean the building. As in Italy, we didn't want to miss any opportunity to develop family ties or be of service. We made neighborhood connections too, and after three months, I'd started babysitting full time—to earn extra money, still be home with the kids, and help out a working mom. One night, on the way home from church, Keith pulled the car over and—in his words—blew up: "It's too much! I can't keep up with everything at work, keep up with everything at church, and spend time with the kids!" I confessed the same feelings. Time had become our enemy.

It *was* too much, so—finally—we gave it to God. Things got better. The New Christians Class ended, Keith and I settled into our jobs, and the newly-developed relationships blossomed into mutual support. This time, those included older, mature Christians. There was Max, the preacher, who'd taught the New Christians Class—lots of great lessons, but the memory that sticks is his "affront" to a few older women in the congregation. Months after the love of his life died, Max went on a Christian Singles cruise and brought back a new wife—lovely to the core. The ladies in his first wife's Bible class weren't as quick to adjust, to which Max replied, "I loved being married so much, I wanted to be married again as soon as possible." What a tribute to wife #1! Then there was Larry, the founder of the attached "Clifton Park School of Preaching." He'd studied at Sunset—just like us! Unlike us— he'd also graduated from it and gone on to plant churches and another school of preaching in New Zealand before founding this one. He and his wife, Helen, were zealous for God's truth, but with gentle and beautiful spirits. I hated Helen at first, because she was a grandmother with a model-like figure. I'd perfected the habits of dieting and cheating by then. Try as I might, though, I could find no arrogance in her, so I resigned to love her. She taught us younger women a lot about parenting. Another wise couple lived in our neighborhood—John and Marilyn. John taught at the school and at church; Marilyn taught ladies' classes in her home. I enjoyed many great Bible studies with her too, but one thing sticks because of its oddity: "If you're depressed, do your floors." Often works for me. Try it! If it doesn't work, at least you'll be depressed with clean floors.

1 Corinthians 8:1 says, "Knowledge puffs up; love builds up." I'd gotten puffy. Through our interactions with these mature Christians, God gave me a pin to let out the hot air. He showed me that love and humility were better fillers.

God gave us another gift when Clifton Park formed a church plant in our neighborhood. We met in our homes, so we only drove to Clifton Park occasionally. We invited our neighbors, of course, but usually it was just about eight to ten of us, not including kiddos. Two of the young men were graduates of the Clifton Park School. Larry found additional financial support for the guys from three churches in the Bible belt. Two of those sent teams of teenagers up to us to help us hold Vacation Bible Schools for the whole community. It was a treat for us to host the teens in our homes.

Michael and Bill were our two young preachers. They and their wives, Terri and Sherry, became great friends of ours. We all had young kids, and so, like our church family in Italy, we spent a good bit of time together. Despite their youth, Michael and Bill taught well through both their messages and their lives. Bill was Larry's son-in-law, so he and Sherry reflected much of Larry's wisdom. Bill fasted every Thursday to spend it studying God's Word. Sherry homeschooled their young son, which was the first we'd heard of that. Michael had been a professional musician but left it when he met Christ. Had to change the lifestyle. He still played piano and accordion, often entertaining seniors at a nearby home. He modeled friendship-making: "How can we grow this relationship?" he asked us. Intentional.

We grew especially close to Michael and Terri. Michael and Keith played tennis regularly; sometimes, we'd join them. We all went camping—once. Michael almost set the forest ablaze, adding gasoline to a slow-burning fire, so we stuck to non-flammable activities after that. Keith and I bought a timeshare in Lake Placid—site of the former Olympics. The purchase was a financial mistake, but I don't regret our time spent sledding with all the kids, watching them all splash around in the huge jacuzzi, and having a fondue dessert in front of the roaring fire (which we supervised), after the kids were in bed.

During a particularly happy time for us, the Keegans joined our church family, as Peter worked in our area on two different occasions. They were with us for much of our slideshow study of Francis Schaffer's book, *How Should We Then Live?*[6], a faith-affirming journey through the history of art, science, and philosophy to see how the west was lost—western civilization, that is—how it lost its base of absolute truth, morality, and values. So fun to have our old friends engage with our new friends, for a study of such significance.

We were in Saratoga Springs from May 1980 to November 1983, and while we'd formed a new family there, we had a sense that something unnaturally familial was developing between my mom and Keith's dad back in Minnesota. Our parents lived less than five miles apart in St. Paul. They'd known each other for the decade of our marriage and communicated regularly, to keep current on our adventures. At the same time, both my dad and Keith's mom suffered chronic conditions— my dad, Alzheimer's; Keith's mom, diabetes. My dad's home had been a nursing home since our time in Italy. Keith's mom, long blind from diabetes, was in and out of the hospital with infections which claimed one foot and threatened to claim the other. So, for years, my mom—an RN—provided support to Keith's parents. Keith's dad, a vehicle mechanic for the state, helped my mom with home or auto repairs. My mom told me of several visits to Keith's mom in the hospital where a nurse begged her to take Keith's dad to dinner or something to get him out of the hospital for a bit.

Their natural support system grew to a deep friendship. Keith's mom passed away on February 11, 1982. She was sixty-one. Keith went home for the funeral. He came back in grief, but with confirmation of what we'd both suspected—my mom and his dad were getting pretty close. Nothing dramatic, just very supportive of the other. They went grocery shopping together, came back laughing, and then made lunch. Since they were together so often, I started addressing letters to "Mom (and dad L)," to save a letter. A year later, when my dad's mind was all but gone, some business with mom's house in Orange City, FL, beckoned her there. Mom was a native Floridian, and her father had left her his house. Keith's dad accompanied her to Florida. We joined them—partly to vacation, partly to chaperone? My dad was still technically alive, and these two acted like an old married couple. Again, no blatant PDAs, but they were...close. Our feelings were conflicted. We'd each thought these two would be a good fit if what seemed inevitable happened—but Mom was still married to my dad. Would we say something to them? What? How would we answer any questions from the kids on the subject? We, I think rightly, concluded it was theirs to work out. I looked at Keith in bed one night and said, "You could be my stepbrother." Ewww—I sidled to the edge of the bed to ponder that.

A month after the Florida trip, my dad died, and I went home for the funeral. I could see the strain on mom's face from the years of suffering she'd endured with my dad's Alzheimer's. My mom and

Keith's dad had gone through such trying times for what seemed an eternity. This time, I was grateful to see them sitting close, with his arm supporting her.

"Teach me knowledge and good judgment, for I trust your commands." Psalm 119:66

CHAPTER SIX

I NOW PRONOUNCE YOU BROTHER AND SISTER

HALLMARK DOESN'T MAKE CARDS FOR THIS. I RAN THE bottom line on my way to Minnesota for their wedding. My husband becomes my stepbrother. My father-in-law becomes stepfather to not only me, but my two older brothers. My mom takes on Keith's sister as stepdaughter. My mom takes on my married name— Mrs. Longtin! Our in-laws will be living together! Too weird.

We were all adults, though, so the weird factor wasn't that contagious—pretty much confined to Keith and me. Keith's family knew them as "dad and Helen." My family knew them as "mom and Vic." To us, they remained "mom and dad," but that definition required some mental adjustment.

Turns out, they refused to be defined by their relationship to any of us. They were two people who had suffered years of grief, who found comfort in the other and were looking ahead, not back. My mom had a mug which I have on my desk here. It says, "Sometimes we have to build our own rainbows." The picture is of a builder, nailing together rainbow-colored pieces of wood. She was always good at making the most of her life and re-inventing herself. I always admired her inner strength. Mom had wondered if she could go through the physical decline of a spouse again but decided if they could get ten good years together, it was worth the plunge.

We didn't know at that time how blessed we all would be through the union of those two, and I won't go into it yet, but again, God had a plan. Stay tuned.

They married on February 25, 1984. I served as mom's matron of honor, and Keith's brother-in-law served as best man. Keith was his dad's only son, but another lady had claim on Keith's time then, so we missed out on a great photo op of the two Longtin couples. The ceremony couldn't have been that memorable, because I don't remember it; I just remember that it was in a room in a church building, and it was just us. At the end of it, they kissed. My mom, Keith's dad. Eeewww.

Mom had just retired. She and Keith's dad sold both of their homes, watched two lifetimes of memorabilia be trucked away and moved to my grandfather's nine-hundred-square-foot home in Orange City, FL—two beds and a bath, no garage, no basement, no AC. OK, maybe *they* deserve the award for biggest adjustment to make.

The lady with dibs on Keith's time was the USS Sand Lance, another fast attack submarine. Her demands on the now-Chief Longtin were just as finicky as those of his last gray lady. When not wandering the deep, Sand Lance harbored in Charleston, SC, and we anchored in Summerville, SC, about twenty-five miles northwest.

There is an upside to a parent marrying an in-law—saves the argument about which parents to visit. With "the folks" just about seven hours away, we saw them more often, when Keith was home. When we went there, we often lazed about on a houseboat on the St. Johns River. No, they didn't buy one; they joined a houseboat club. Keith's dad (or just "dad" now, I'm reminded) loved to fish, and mom loved anything on the water. Dad let us take turns at the helm—even the kids— when we weren't in danger of hitting anything.

When mom and dad came to our place, we toured Charleston, the museum, the straw market, plantations—they both loved history. One visit for them, though, proved historic in a way we'd all like to forget. Keith and I decided to celebrate our eleventh anniversary in Hawaii. Mom and dad accepted our offer to enjoy quality time with their grandchildren in our home for that week (you have to frame these things just right). Like we do when you and Lukas come for a visit, Lucy, I'm sure they excitedly made plans for all kinds of fun activities. Diana, however, brewed up ideas of her own. In Hawaii, we watched helplessly as that hurricane, the first major one to hit the east coast in twenty years, had them in her sights. Mom and dad scrambled to secure the fort and race the neighbors for the last of the hurricane supplies. On their way out one day, mom asked Renée to close and lock the sliding glass door. Renée was usually one to submit to authority, but apparently at that moment, she'd had enough and responded with, "Why do I have to do everything around here?!" My mom swatted her backside. Now, in my book, Renée got off easy, because if I'd said that twenty years earlier, my options would have been a mouthful of Ivory soap or a hairbrush applied to my bare bottom as I balanced over mom's knees. Renée didn't see it that way. To her seven-year-old mind, grandma just morphed from Glinda the good witch to the wicked witch of the west.

Renée's recounting of that incident brought me back to a similar humiliation I'd suffered as a seven-year-old. It was at the house in Orange City, then occupied by my grandpa and step-grandmother. We were on vacation, and I was meeting them for the first time. After I'd established some rapport with my grandpa, I crawled up in his lap. Step-grandmother yelled from the kitchen, "Get off of him; you might hurt him!" Yikes! I quickly crawled down from his lap and kept my distance from her. Cinderella's stepmother, in spotted, wrinkly flesh. That overwrote the happier memories of their taking us to Marineland and Silver Springs.

Years later, she mailed me a shoebox of fabric scraps. My friends, who were experienced in receiving gifts from grandparents, thought it lame. Not me; I loved to sew Barbie clothes, and she'd found out. Our brief relationship improved.

(Lucy, if I ever say or do anything that causes you or Lukas offense, talk to me! Before you, I'd never been a grandparent. I don't want to mess this up!)

During that time with the kids, Renée and Hurricane Diana weren't alone in testing mom's nerves. Dad had a stroke the same week. One of our dogs jumped in to protect him from the paramedics, barking and snarling at the intruders, so assistance was perilous. We talked to mom on the phone a couple of times, but we couldn't get home because of the storm. Fortunately—at least for us, Diana moved to North Carolina, and dad recovered well. The only residual was Renée's wariness of her grandma, which—like the storm, dissipated over time.

Our house in South Carolina was one of my favorites—it was visually warm, with a huge fireplace in the living room, burnt orange carpet, and all wood frame. Another creature found the wood frame a favorite—a woodpecker who regularly serenaded us as he hammered at a knot. We named him Woody, but called him other names too.

When Keith was at sea, I became a pyromaniac—loved to build a fire and just get lost in the flames. Quiet serenity and contemplation. One evening a week, our home hosted a Bible study group, whether or not Keith was there. They encouraged me when he wasn't, helped me stay focused on God rather than my problems or loneliness. I remember setting up the VCR [Google it] to record *Scarecrow and Mrs. King* before the group started—my favorite TV show at the time. I've always been a sucker for romance with a shallow plot.

Keith had little solace or encouragement on the submarine, so his at-sea times were lonelier for him, even though he shared life with one hundred guys in a sardine can. He did get to visit England and spend a day or two in London. On a northern run, he earned his "Order of the Blue Nose" award when the boat crossed the Arctic Circle, and he survived the obligatory hazing-style "ceremony."

One fall weekend scared Keith out of his wits, but this time, it wasn't the boat's fault. He'd pulled into port and tried to call us. Mom, dad, the kids, and I had all gone to Greenville, SC, to see fall color and get some apples. Our car broke down, which delayed us a few days there. Keith called day and night and was worried sick when I didn't answer. Remember, no cell phones—landline only. Usually, we wives heard through the boat's phone tree when the boat would be in port, but before we left, I hadn't heard. If I had, I wouldn't have left the house. Thanks be to God, we got home before the boat sailed, so he didn't have to take his fears with him.

As usual, our closest friends there were from church. We had our group, but I met Jo, admin for the church, in a ladies' Bible class. I respected her comments in class and then asked her outright if she'd like to be friends. That's something of a risk, I know, but she agreed and we hung out—mostly at our house. Sometimes, she helped me with my Sunday school class; once, she even went with me and the kids to visit the folks in Florida, while Keith was at sea. I learned a lot from Jo, but maybe the most memorable was to never speak ill of your spouse to others. She was able to practice that even when her marriage struggled.

Through friends from church, I found two part-time jobs. One friend owned a nursery—plants, not kids—and needed seasonal help for a while. Once that gig ended, another friend needed help in her TMH (Trainable Mentally Handicapped) class at the local elementary school. I volunteered in her class and then for another teacher. Finally, I became a substitute teacher for the local school district. Quite honestly, I prayed every morning I wouldn't get called, but God answered most of those prayers, "No," and I stayed fairly busy. At least I was home when my kids were home.

My passion was to teach Sunday school—second grade. They don't have the "attitude" yet of the third graders, but they've lost the "deer in the headlights" look of first graders. It was about that time that I was influenced by two books by Lawrence Richards[7]. In them, he described children as "experiencers" rather than sponges that absorb and spew out facts. How does an eight-year-old understand, "Jesus was the perfect lamb of God who died on the cross and whose blood washed away the sins of the world?" What goes through the poor kid's mind as he cuddles his stuffed lamb? If we cram religious terminology down a kid's throat, does that lead to an adult who's better at rote than relationship? From such thoughts, I wrote and taught my own curriculum for the first time. I started with what a child needs to know (and can understand) about Jesus's love and brought in related scripture. I created lessons to interact with the child's senses—acted out stories, had them retell what they heard, used interactive visual aids. The most effective method of teaching Christ is always the home, as parents model their faith and talk about Him along the way, but teachers must make the most of the minutes they have every week.

The leadership of any congregation must be on board with teachers who think they know better than the commercial curriculum, and ours gave me the benefit of the doubt. As our time in South Carolina came to an end, I felt so excited about this method of teaching, I couldn't wait to share it with a new leadership team in Florida. Surely any new church would embrace us and my ideas.

"Open my eyes that I may see wonderful things in
your law." Psalm 119:18

CHAPTER SEVEN

"ROYCE, I'VE GOT HER!"

SUNDAY MORNING SERVICE HAD JUST ENDED AT Concord St. Church when an elder stopped me in the center aisle. He yelled to another elder in the outside aisle, "Royce, I've got her!" When Royce joined us, they interrogated me: "We heard you had your second grade Sunday school class to your house for lunch and mixed bathing."

"Mixed bathing...uh..." They recognized the blank gaze on my face.

"Girls and boys swimming together." Yes, it was true—most of the class, Keith, myself, and another couple were all in the pool. That was...inappropriate? The elders were nice about it, but I got the message: don't do that again.

In New York, our church group often went to the lake after service for a picnic lunch and swim, so I didn't get it, but I opted for a pizza party the next time I had my class over. We were at this Orlando church because they were well-established, and we'd heard of their good works in the community. If they wanted communion servers to wear a tie, or kids' shorts to be a certain length at camp, we'd accommodate. Churches are made up of humans, so the perfect congregation can only be found in heaven. This one had an active youth program. With Jake and Renée headed into the traumatic middle and high school years, that was important to us. We'd visited a church closer to our new home in Oviedo but they were too young to have such a program. In hindsight, we think it might have been better to work with the group that was in our neighborhood. Interesting note for later chapters though—the young church had just hired a young preacher named Dan Holland, whom they expected shortly. Pay attention to the name; you'll see it again in later chapters.

I learned right away that my Sunday school philosophy differed from my supervisor, and with no need to ask. The evidence jumped off her classroom walls. Enthroned in laminated poster board were ALL the kings of Israel and Judah, from the some-two hundred years of the divided kingdom. Not only were they to be memorized, but characterized. They were labeled, "evil, good, mostly good, or mostly evil." Her husband had created an impressive tabletop tabernacle to scale, completely furnished. No discussion necessary. I walked out thinking, "Her fifth-graders will be well-prepared for Bible Bowl, but what about life?" In order to continue to teach, I tried to merge our goals and keep quiet about mine. I'm not sure I succeeded at the latter. When she declared her intent to retire as supervisor of the elementary program, the elders asked me to take the position. I agreed. She decided not to retire.

As an adult, I love to incorporate her style in my own study. We appreciated the historical detail brought in by the intense study of our teachers at Concord. One thing I miss about our contemporary church is the lack of adult Sunday school. I still love in-depth Bible studies that haul out all available references, but those aren't as easy to come by in modern churches. I do it on my own, of course, but my self-discipline tends to work best with the crutch of accountability. Concord made that time on a Sunday morning. Hmm...maybe I'll start such a group! There's an idea!

For our first few years in Oviedo, Keith was on shore duty. He was an instructor at the Navy's Nuclear Field "A" School in Orlando (which is no longer there). He liked to teach, and we loved having him home. He drove the church van on Sundays and Wednesdays, to pick up his favorite people—the elderly, mostly women. They'd laugh and tease—made his day, and theirs. In 1990, Keith had to go to sea again for two years—his last two years in the navy. He was able to get a billet for another submarine home-ported in Charleston. This time he was stationed on the USS Calhoun, an "FBM," or "Fleet Ballistic Missile" submarine. An FBM stays at sea most of the time, so it has two crews, switching off every three months. We kept our home in Oviedo, and Keith drove the seven hours home from Charleston on weekends when his crew was in port. I always wanted our home to be in Keith's home port, but with the boat out for six months anyway, we made an exception. We didn't want to move the kids again in their middle/high school years and didn't want to be farther from our aging parents. After praying about it, we chose Oviedo for our permanent home port.

Early in our years in Florida, I took on two new enterprises—went back to school and started a cleaning business. I wanted a degree in Educational Psychology, with the thought to influence Sunday school curriculum. With only nine credits in my pocket from my younger days, it'd be a long road. I phoned my friend Jo with my doubts: "I'll be an old lady by the time I get a degree!"

She responded, "You'll be an old lady anyway; may as well be one with a degree." Too true.

The cleaning biz idea came from our minister's wife, who had such a business. I've never been accused of keeping a spotless home, so Barbara allowed me to tag along and learn from her. My own home appreciated it. Who knew that cupboard tops needed attention? (I'm convinced that's why fashionable cupboards now meet the ceiling.) I advertised locally and got a couple of houses. Other than a little breakage here and there, I guess I was either really good or really cheap, as referrals pushed me up to ten or twelve homes a week. Work was my workout, so the job saved a gym membership.

I tried to be home when the kids were. They were growing independent, but moms need to be needed, so at first, I just dabbled at community college. I soon decided I'd have to ramp up if I wanted to graduate before the turn of *my* century, so had to get creative with my schedule. There were some mornings I'd clean half a house, go to class, and then come back to finish it—whatever worked.

Keith and I found ourselves in the sandwich generation. Dad's health worsened—he had a couple of strokes and a brain shunt, so mom and dad were more and more stuck in Orange City. They made the effort to join us at Christmas, but other than that, we went up there. By the mid-nineties, we went up every Sunday to run errands with mom.

We took a couple of memorable trips before Jake and Renée left home—one to our timeshare in Lake Placid, NY, the other to Helen, Georgia. You know my Cabbage Patch doll, Luther? Well,

I "adopted" him at the "Baby-land General Hospital" in Cleveland, Georgia, on that latter trip. The whole rest of the trip, Renée pretended to annoy me by tossing him around like a TOY instead of the toddler that he was! I played my part and acted annoyed. The highlight of that trip, though, was a long hike down a fall-covered circular path that turned out not to be circular. As it grew dark, we realized we couldn't backtrack to the car. After some moments of silent panic, God provided a vehicle with an angel of a driver, who took us back. The lowlight of the trip was that Jake sliced his finger while cooking. We drove almost an hour at night to find a hospital to stitch him up.

When she wasn't abusing cloth toddlers, Renée worked hard—graduated third in her class in high school and went on to earn her degree in chemical engineering from UF. Jacob worked hard too, but college wasn't in his future yet. Developmental dyslexia made high school—and too often home—miserable. We didn't know about the dyslexia until recently, so our "You can do this!" mantra and efforts to help with homework only served to further his frustration. When it comes to visual learning, Jake's in the top 1 percent of the nation—he can reproduce a complicated design after looking at it for only a minute. Unfortunately, public schools don't teach that way. After high school, he followed in his father's footsteps and joined the submarine force. (Keith is 5'6", so he tried to tell him he'd get stuck in the hatches with his 6'1" frame, but he still went). Jake served our country for fourteen years and learned compensatory skills. He not only finished college, but got his master's degree. Like Renée, he married a loving Godly spouse who complements his character. We couldn't be prouder of both our kids—not because they've "succeeded" in life, but have pure hearts.

They seek God's will for their lives and do their best to obey it. I probably don't say it often enough, but I'm crazy about 'em both.

After Keith retired from the navy, he and I served on the missions' committee at Concord. The church sent us to Caracas to meet with Beto, a local preacher who'd been mentored by our American missionary and was now ready to take over, when our missionary returned to Texas. Keith and I were two of a group of Venezuelan church supporters from all over the states. We landed in Caracas. Hillsides filled with shanties. Poverty everywhere. People either had money or they didn't—not really a middle class. Keith and I met with Beto and another preacher. Between Beto's broken English and my broken Spanish, we all bonded instantly. They and the twenty-five or so of us Americans took an embarrassingly nice bus through poor towns on our way to Puerto La Cruz/ Barcelona, where we'd meet with other congregations. Children ran from all around to see this luxury bus on their dirt roads. We were invited to a home with a dirt floor, two or three rooms occupied by multiple generations. Some of us sat outside, some stood. Our hostess made sure we all had something to drink. It was made with water, so another American refused to drink it. The rest of us drank it; I would rather have gotten sick than offend.

We marveled at the local Christians' zeal and determination. They faced challenges you and I have never known (yet), but their confidence in God oozed from them like sweat. They didn't speak of baby showers, potluck luncheons, or even what visual aids to use for Sunday School. They discussed safe places to meet together, how best to interact with government officials who demanded bribes, and their conversations with Christian married men reluctant to part with their mistresses. They didn't just face corrupt government and cultural practices, but daily violence. On our way home, we learned that our sweet bus driver for the week had just been shot and killed. He was up on his roof, adjusting an antenna. Probably just target practice from a passing vehicle, they said. Not uncommon. We were stunned.

As a result of that trip, we had a handful of opportunities to host our Venezuelan friends in our home. They'd come up for a missions' forum or one of the "Spiritual Growth Workshops" that Concord was known for. Their visits always re-energized our faith.

The Venezuela trip was March 1994. Jake went to boot camp that year and then to sub school in Groton, Connecticut. In 1995, Renée went off to UF.

We had an empty nest for about two years, before mom and dad became the second Mr. and Mrs. Longtin in the household. But before we get into that timeframe, I have to give you the "gray side" of the years I've just described. When Satan sees you drawing closer to Christ, you can bet he's prowling around you. He found a chink in my armor. So much so that I've sometimes called the years I've just described, my "atheist years."

"I seek you with all my heart; do not let me stray from your commands." Psalm 119:10

CHAPTER EIGHT

LOVING THE LORD WITH HALF MY MIND

AS I WRITE THIS, LUCY, YOU AND LUKAS ARE HAVING TO "home school" again because of the coronavirus pandemic. Nobody has ever seen anything like this that has affected so many so quickly. Nobody that is, except God—He's not surprised by anything, and He's not only seen something like this, but has hated it from the beginning. I refer to sin. As I read about how the coronavirus attacks the body, it reminds me of the insidiousness and gravity of sin.

Just as the coronavirus can disguise itself so that the body doesn't recognize it as an intruder, so sin masks itself and stays hidden until it finds a good point to attack. So far, I've tried to describe how my faith grew strong—not just through study, but through God's vivid work in our lives. Despite that experience of

His presence, I started to ask if He even exists. Dumb, right?! I know! But sin is that deceitful.

The coronavirus has spikes on its exterior that "look for" matching human cells it can attach to, like jigsaw puzzle pieces. It favors the respiratory cells, especially the delicate lung cells—those most vulnerable. Sin also looks for the most vulnerable point of entry. The Enemy didn't attack my inspiring experience with the Venezuelans or my passion for teaching children. He didn't attack truth, but feelings—my self-concept. He massaged the lie he'd deeply implanted that told me, "Compared to almost anybody else, you don't measure up—in smarts, wit, creativity, discipline, you name it." My faith usually informed my feelings, but this time, low self-esteem's cousin Pride showed up to create doubt.

In this case, is was my return to college that afforded the Enemy that opportunity. Some of my professors not-so-subtly inferred that those who held Christian beliefs in the twentieth century were either dangerously deranged or deserved a condescending pat on the head and a one-way ticket to someplace safe and out of sight. Said professors brimmed with authoritative self-confidence, and I envied that. Even when I disagreed with the premises on which their arguments were based, the insecure cells in my soul fell victim to the virus of doubt. I started reading books by more liberal theologians, Jews, and atheists. God fed my mind and soul as described in the previous chapter, but to be "objective" while I read, I told Him to wait outside while I figured out if He was really there or a figment of my desire. I questioned my faith instead of hauling the doubt into an interrogation room with a penetrating light. My mind led a dual life. I was His one minute but then thought, *But what if?* I wrote to our experienced missionary in Venezuela with questions because I didn't trust the influence of anyone local—on either side. His validation of my struggle, book suggestions, and insightful specific answers reassured me and my faith. Still, I allowed my mind to waver back and forth. Don't get me wrong—I think it's most reasonable to examine what you believe, but I'd done that to my satisfaction. I'd even concluded that I didn't have enough faith to be an atheist. I knew enough to love God with ALL my mind, heart, and soul. Still, some part of me very gradually began the downward slither into that arrogance that crowns oneself an Intellectual.

With all the reading that you do, Lucy, you must know Hans Christian Andersen's story, "The Emperor's New Clothes"[8]? To summarize, two swindlers convince all the nobles and townspeople that only those of high intelligence can see the magnificent clothing they design for the emperor. No one wants to confess that they have less than superior intellect and so all praise the rich colors, intricate design, and lavish features of the clothes they don't see. That goes on until finally a child points out what everyone sees—the emperor, parading down the street, has nothing on! Like those nobles, I didn't want to admit that I could see nothing in my professors' judgements. Why did I allow this ping-pong agony to continue for so long?! Looking back, I can relate to Ralphie in *A Christmas Story*[9], when he's pulled off Santa's lap. He starts to slide down and realizes he didn't ask Santa for the Red Ryder BB gun that he wants. He screams to himself, "Wake Up, Stupid!" If I could talk to younger me at this time, that's what I'd want to scream.

I would not discuss any doubt with Jake or Renée nor change anything in my lifestyle unless I could confidently embrace atheism, because of its logically hopeless conclusions: If there is no God, I'm a random act of chance. If that's true, I have every reason to question the validity of my perception of reality and my own thought processes. If there is nothing outside ourselves, there is no absolute truth, so "truth" is whatever the majority decides it to be. If there is no absolute truth, "right" and "wrong," "good" and "evil" are meaningless terms. If I'm just an accident of nature, my life has no inherent purpose and, of course, death is the end. Still, like the atheists—if I could conclude that God doesn't exist, I would accept those logical conclusions. Yes, I questioned my thought processes on this subject as I would have to do on all others, but if a well-educated atheist could reach this humanist proclamation, I'd try to keep an open mind.

Some Sundays, I taught Sunday school with all my usual creativity, came downstairs for the service, and thought, *Boy, these people are gullible.* Following Keith's time at sea, he retired from the navy, and I hosted a retirement party for him. I asked one of the church elders, a former naval officer named Chuck, to speak at it. As I wrote out the invitations, I wondered, *What would Chuck think, if he knew I didn't believe in God?*

When God opens a door to your mind, it's to reveal Himself. When Satan opens a door to your mind, he's holding it open for sin. Like the virus that uses the cell's machinery to replicate, sin used my low self-concept to mutate my arrogance into the self-righteousness that thrives by imagining weakness in others. This time, it threatened our marriage. You'll remember that Keith retired from the navy after his last two years of sea duty. Now, he lived at home permanently for the first time in our marriage. We'd always adjusted to new roles after his being at sea, but this time, I expected him to merge into our world as if he'd been there the whole time. His actions were never enough, nor the right ones. Yes, he drove us long miles every week to be at church whenever it was open, ushered, drove the church van, and served on the missions team. But he didn't take over the spiritual leadership of our family or pursue a title. I thought he should have come off the boat fully equipped with the instinct and my know-how to conduct regular family devotions. And, I expected him to work his way up the church ladder to deacon at least, if not elder. I called a meeting with him to "share our expectations of our marriage." He had no idea what this was about, so I went first. After I read my list of expectations, he was crying. Annoyed, I asked why. "I just wanted to make you happy!" was his response. That's my husband's character, through and through, but at the time, his response just made me more frustrated. What do you do with THAT, when you're trying to fix somebody?!

Sin continued to replicate the self-righteousness. My soul's consciousness tried to point out the sin and battle back, but pride fought back hard. Frustration with one's spouse (or anyone else) gives you new lenses. They blind you to the good in the other but magnify even the tiniest irritant. These visual distortions grow exponentially if not checked. With my perceptions thus skewed, my brain was battle-weary and yearned for relief. Enter a flashy smile and quick wit outside of the marriage, and the sinful mind has a welcome distraction. My thoughts and emotions found comfort in the shallow companionship of another. Nothing physical ever happened, but I created opportunity to spend time, and that's lust, which the Bible labels as adulterous.

Keith questioned my activity, but I got defensive and accused him of impure suspicion. All he could do was let me work it out alone—or he hoped, with God. Keith knew I questioned my faith; we talked about it. He never questioned God's existence. If he questioned anything, it was just what the church should look like.

I should never have allowed the baseless doubt its voice for all that time. Nevertheless, that internal agony resulted in a faith that can't now be shaken. I'm just grateful that God held me in His cupped hands while I struggled—and gave me a husband who loves me as He does.

Before I leave this chapter, I have to include a beautiful and reassuring poem that a dear lady in our small group wrote for me, after I finally confessed the faith struggle to them. Beautifully framed, it remains on my dresser today. God spoke to me through her words:

Faith

Why O God did you create my mind so full of doubt,
To struggle and to wonder what you are all about?
Why can't my faith be simple, as others' faith can be,
An ability to believe without the logic to see?
Do you really exist beyond all space and time,
Or has my religion been just a waste of time?
I want to believe you, God, I want to know you are there,
Please guide my thoughts and let me know I am in your care.

"You, my child, are special, a rare jewel on my throne,
You have the gift of reason, not many have ever known.
Don't look at this gift as a curse that drives me away,
For it's through this gift that I will use you in a special way.
Your struggle and your pain are the only way I can be,
The part of your life that you need for me to be.
For through the storms of your doubt, there will come a glow,
A serenity and peace that you now long to know.
Let me live inside your heart, where I long to be,
Then others who have doubt can my glory see."

by Ginger Broslat, 1996

I can't read her work without tears, because I have now realized that glow, serenity, and peace. That's why I'm writing this memoir—because Napa and I so wish those for you and Lukas.

I'm getting ahead of myself, because you two weren't you two yet. The two that would most affect the next years of our life were mom and dad, who came to live with us in 1997. Loose threads from the struggle in this chapter will come together in the next two, before a new struggle begins. Struggles with God, in my experience, usually make one's faith stronger. Struggles with sin are like fighting the coronavirus without a vaccine or treatment. Sin has to be taken to the Great Physician. His Word is the vaccine, and Christ is the cure.

"All your words are true; all your righteous laws are eternal." Psalm 119:160

CHAPTER NINE

WHICH MR. AND MRS. LONGTIN?

THE PHONE RINGS. I PICK IT UP. "IS THIS MRS. LONGTIN?"

"Maybe—which one do you want—Mrs. Kathy Longtin, or Mrs. Helen Longtin?"

"Uh...." on the other end. When Keith's dad (now just "dad," remember) and my mom moved in with us, the confusion of outsiders amused us. Such small amusements brought relief to this communal life we'd chosen.

I'm sure I don't have to tell you, Lucy, that mother-daughter relationships can be a little like life in a bounce house. From my experience, the drama lessens when the daughter leaves home. Well, there is that period where one might sit on the daughter's bed, hug the unused pillow, and wail. But after that, again from my experience, the other becomes your best friend. If you have to move back into the same kitchen again, well...then there's the question, "Will the cord that binds feel more like a tightrope?"

In early 1997, we had opportunity to test that when we saw the need. Dad's health continued to decline, and our Sunday visits were not enough. We decided to sell both our homes and move in together. With palatial visions in my head, we shopped large new homes spacious enough for not only the four of us, but for Jake and Renée when they visited. In the end, Keith and mom wisely decided that mom and dad move in to our current house—all 1,690 square feet of it. I was deflated, but outvoted, so I adjusted.

We unstapled the mass of Garfield comics that personalized Jake's walls, painted the room a bland green, and rented a hospital bed with tray table. That became dad's room. We cleared out all remnants of Renée from her room and replaced her—I mean them—with mom's belongings. To me, our nest hadn't been empty all that long. Jake enlisted three years earlier and lived on the submarine USS Pittsburgh. Renée was a senior at UF and did internships in Macon, GA. Still, I felt as if I'd just locked the door behind them. On their return visits to their childhood home, they were displaced to sleep on a pull-out couch or an air mattress. They adjusted graciously, if not easily.

We welcomed mom and dad with flowers and cards, and the move-in process went smoothly. Don't even get Keith started on the move-out process. Mom, like others who went through the Great Depression, had little use for a trash can. They'd already squeezed the lifetime collections of two "forever homes" into 900 square feet. Now, she had to funnel that further to fit just two bedrooms. We truly wanted her to make those decisions, but there came a point we had to step in. On one Sunday visit before the move, she said she'd worked all week to pack items we could move in. The result was a shoebox on the kitchen table. Once we ensured they had the necessities of life in our house, Chief Longtin took command. Every night after work, Keith drove the forty-five minutes home; swallowed supper; drove the hour to their house; and then packed, cleaned, and painted the house to get it on the market. That included the backyard shed. Untouched in years, it was stuffed to the brim with mildewed, unrecognizable items that had served as home to communities of roaches and mice—at least. When he finished, not much was left. After they moved in with us, every time mom couldn't find something, she concluded, "Keith probably threw it away (sigh)." He probably did.

This joint venture had to work. Think of the dynamics, the consequences if any two of us couldn't get along. The material was ripe for even a lackluster sitcom writer, but we were interdependent. Keith's dad, soon bedridden, was totally dependent on mom's nursing skills. Mom depended on me for transferring him, transportation, and keeping the house. We all depended on Keith for income and his ability to fix anything broken—be it house, car, or peace.

So, we all brought our best for the team. It wasn't hard for Keith and his dad, blessed with sanguine personalities. That, and dad's strokes had left him speechless, so he could only communicate with his famed smile that said not just, "Hi, how ya doin'?" but "I'm so happy to see you!!" Even mom and I strove to be on our best behavior. It's not like we had a bad relationship—it was close, and living apart, we were very good friends. Her support had been invaluable during Keith's deployments. Beyond emotional support, she often drove with me from one home port to the next and watched the kids while I shopped for a home. We were just different, and she had the dominant personality. As the oldest of two children, she'd had to grow up quickly when their mother left home. A young teenager at the time, she managed schoolwork, her younger brother, and her alcoholic father. She left their Florida home at just nineteen to attend nurses' training in Minnesota—a bold move in 1939. She was always a strong woman and a people person, fitting a Jane Austen character's description of "good company": "My idea of good company, Mr Elliot, is the company of clever, well-informed people, who have a great deal of conversation; that is what I call good company."[10] That was my mom.

I envied that about her; I'm shy by nature. I sought her approval. I'm sure I always had it, but I didn't always feel sure of it for a couple of reasons. One, I was the youngest; my brothers were seven and nine years older, so my early contributions to family conversation were never well-enough informed. That, and I was a replacement kid. My parents had always wanted a girl but stopped trying after their third boy. The five of them came down from Minnesota to visit relatives in Florida in 1952. I have a couple of pictures from that trip. One shows the three brothers—Chuck, Jim, and Petey. In matching shirts, they sit on boxes and fish from a dock. The dock was at my mom's aunt's house on Lake Rowena, in Orlando. The other picture was taken that night at a family picnic. My grandpa, cigarette in hand, studies the newest grandson on his lap with apparent approval. Petey, four and a half, smiles broadly to the camera. The next morning, Petey got up before the family and went back to the dock. They found one shoe on the dock, so they theorized that maybe the other fell in the water and he'd tried to retrieve it. First responders found his body in the lake. With massive support from their church back home, my parents brought the family back to Minnesota. In the midst of their terrible grief, our parents decided to try again for a girl, and I came along less than a year later. The whole family was still scarred for life in some way. Even though I wasn't born when Petey drowned, that includes me, as I heard the story often retold. My early conclusions were: 1) water is dangerous and 2) if Petey were here, I wouldn't be, so therefore, I shouldn't be.

Even as an adult who knew better than to draw that conclusion, I sometimes wondered, *How would things be different if he were here? What would he be doing? What do they expect of this long-awaited girl?*

Lucy, I still don't know the answers to those questions, and I no longer need to, but I know that if I wasn't here, your mother wouldn't be here. If your beautiful mother wasn't here, you and Lukas wouldn't be here. And, for the record, Napa and I are VERY happy you're here!

So, it was my nature to want my mom's approval and to second-guess possession of it even if expressed. One day, as we chattered and prepared dad for the day, she enlightened me a little: "Don't take everything I say personally. Usually, I'm just speaking as a person, not your mother." My intellect spoon-fed that concept to my inner child. My mother—a person separate from that role? Not everything she said had a reference to me? Hmmm... Once I digested that, most of my gut-level sensitivity eased up, and it released me to be more her friend. We even made special time at 3:00 every day—to watch reruns of *Scarecrow and Mrs. King* with cappuccino.

I need to mention the fifth person in the house, who made our foursome work. I joyfully give God the credit for His work as peacemaker. We implored Him constantly for those attitude-adjustment procedures He does so well. My faith was stronger; I'll speak of that in the next chapter. Mom hadn't attended church in years but was on intimate terms with Jesus. With God's help, Keith and I were determined to meet our parents' needs or wants as best we could. Rick Warren said, "Humility is not thinking less of yourself, but thinking of yourself less."[11] With both our wills and energies dedicated to serving our parents in this way, we experienced how love inhibits self-indulgent thought.

They'd moved in with us in June of 1997. I still had one semester and an internship to finish up, so it wasn't until the next summer that I could be home with them full-time, but that time-line worked out well and gave us an adjustment period. I ended my cleaning business in December 1997. Mom and dad's help with financial expenses allowed me to stay home to be at their beck and call. Keith had also gone back to school but finished his AA degree before they moved in. He still worked full-time in Orlando as a veterans' rep for Jobs and Benefits.

Even though mom was a nurse, home health care workers visited regularly. They were all impressed at the set-up we had. Of course, they didn't see our challenges. Mom had to put up with me and had long lost the ability to converse with her husband. Keith had to manage two fickle women's demands. It was initially awkward for me to attend to my father-in-law's personal care. But the health care workers were right—it was an impressive arrangement, authored by God.

It's such a challenge these days to know how to handle a parent's "golden years" when they can no longer take care of themselves. When do you step in—when you find their keys in the refrigerator, or when they forget what their keys are for? Do you bring them into your nest after it's finally empty? Could you find a facility that will provide high-quality care on a budget? If so, do you choose one close to you or in their own community, far, far away? Home health, maybe? Which ones? Is it safe for mom to be alone when they're not there?

Our circumstances were unique, and I'm sure there are few scenarios as favorable as ours. We, and I think they, were truly blessed. We considered it a tremendous honor to be able to care for them, if imperfectly, for the years they were with us. I don't know how Petey might have responded to the situation, but I'm grateful to God that He placed me there for mom when she needed me the most. As you'll see next, I also needed her. Again.

"Your statutes are my heritages forever; they are the joy of my heart." Psalm 119:111

Chapter Ten

DECISION MADE...AND MADE AGAIN

LUCY, WE OLDER ADULTS OFTEN FEEL A CALL TO A CER-tain room in the middle of the night. When we stay at your house, that involves going upstairs. In the dark, so as not to wake the other, we ascend hesitantly, hang on to the handrail, extend a foot to find each next step, and then grope for the door at the top of the steps. We feel for the doorknob and turn it quietly, so as not to wake Sequoia, asleep in her crate. In contrast, in the light of day, we walk confidently by sight.

God almost blinded my mind with daylight at a Spiritual Growth Workshop in 1996. His Spirit used a speaker's words at the conference to make me finally interrogate my doubt instead of my faith. I don't remember the trigger, but I wrestled all night, in review. I scanned each category of my mind's "Christian Evidences" files to find the source of the doubt. Even if I took the complexity of the universe out of it, I could find no reason for the doubt on literary, philosophical, archeological, or historical grounds. I went back to the beginning—of the doubt, that is. That's where I found it: my insecurities (those lies that Satan tells you about yourself) collided with the well-honed inferences of the opposing worldview. I saw the doubt for what it was—a trust in manmade knowledge that is subjective, instead of trust in the knowledge revealed by the Maker of the Universe, that provides absolute truth, definition, purpose, and meaning to the created world. God removed my veil of arrogant humanism so I could see how foolish I'd been. I suddenly felt utter disdain for the years I'd allowed doubt to stowaway in my brain. I repented at the Sunday morning service following the conference. I re-committed to serve Christ and Him alone. These words by Hillsong exactly express how I felt:

> *Your light broke through my night*
> *Restored exceeding joy*
> *Your grace fell like the rain*
> *And made this desert live*
> *You have turned my mourning into dancing*
> *You have turned my sorrow into joy.*[12]

At once, I wanted to write a letter to the elders—not out of any duty, but to confess to them my too-long internal struggle and to let them share in God's victory and the joy that I couldn't contain. I used a letter instead of verbal communication, so they would read it together at their upcoming meeting. I hoped my enlightenment might encourage them as well. I couldn't wait for their responses.

They didn't respond. The letter didn't really require a response, but I still expected it from the shepherds of our flock. And they weren't just my shepherds, but my friends. We'd served together and been in fellowship for years. I looked for a quick acknowledgment or knowing glance as we passed in the halls. Nothing. After three weeks or so, Keith and I started to wonder about our church's motto, "Where your heart has a home." We weren't sure of that, anymore. We loved so many people there—all true servants of God, but not hearing ANYthing from my elders/brothers about something SO significant to me...well, hurt. Elders have a tangled mass of issues to straighten out, so I've long ago forgiven this oversight, but at the time, I wanted to collect my toys and go elsewhere.

You may remember that we'd visited another church when we moved to Oviedo—one that was closer to us. At the time of that visit, they expected a new minister, one Dan Holland. After our visit, the church kept growing out of places to meet, so they had to name it "Metropolitan" or "Metro" for short. We decided to check it out again. After a few visits, we sought membership, and I resigned my teaching post at Concord. Metro sent a couple of elders to talk. That's when we found out their belief about baptism didn't align with the one that prompted us to get re-baptized in Italy. I have to now confess with embarrassment that I even called this Dan Holland to ask, "Do you know what one of your elders believes?!" Of course, he did. He even managed to explain further, without laughing at the question. Still, we believed the difference to be "of great doctrinal import"[13] at the time.

So, sheepishly, we went back to our old church. I even asked about my teaching position, but that had been filled. One of the elders cleared the air a bit as he noted that all of the elders had been touched by my letter and there were even tears from a few of the five. I wished—at the time—they'd told me. But God had a plan. A dear, wise couple who had earlier made the move from our old church to Metro asked one of the Metro elders to bring us a book on re-baptism. He did— with admitted nervousness, lest we think him too pushy. We studied that book and others in light of scripture. After much prayer, discussion, and study, we did move our membership to Metro.

Fast forward a year or so. Our parents now live with us. Mom, the extravert, quickly begins to thirst for more companionship than we can provide. Every week in the bulletin we bring home from Metro, she sees the name of Carol Darling, office manager. Mom thought Carol a candidate to help her with socialization. I'd barely met Carol, so I deflected the request to contact her, saying that Carol was likely very busy. One Sunday afternoon, Keith stayed with dad while mom and I attended a special music program at Metro. Carol came up and introduced herself to mom. Mom was delighted to meet her and spoke of her request. I all but shrank under my chair at mom's boldness. Carol jumped in with both feet. She took mom out to lunch shortly thereafter and then lined up other women to do the same. Actually, mom always paid, but was very happy to, in return for their time, transportation, and companionship. Mom always came back from lunch speaking of her new friends in glowing terms and recharged by the outings. A few of them came in to chat after they brought her home. I didn't know any of them at the time and found myself judgmental of them, for insanely shallow reasons. Again, I reacted arrogantly as I had when I'd questioned my faith. What was happening?! At the same time, I questioned the outward expressiveness of Metro members. Some raised their hands during a song or prayer; that was new to me. I overheard one man excitedly tell another of a men's conference he'd been to the night before. The whole stadium of men—a species not known for expressiveness—had at one point shouted, "Jesus, Jesus, Jesus!" Could faith be knowledge-centered if it carried this much emotion? My mind conjured up images of TV "prophets" who sell miracle water. Didn't seem genuine to me. I looked down on them too. Satan wasn't done with me yet.

On the way to our Bible study group one evening, Keith had a very unusual outburst. "Everything you say to me is patronizing or condescending." He went on, but that's the summary statement. We sat in the car across the street from the house where our group was about to meet. We argued. I got defensive; he stood his ground. It took time, but his statement eventually sunk in. Not that night, by any means. As couples do, we met with our group as if nothing had happened.

One afternoon, after one of mom's lunch cronies left, I sat in the study and gazed at my soul in the mirror. Who had I become? What characterized me? Judgmentalism? Did I have to pull others down to build myself up? I turned to the book of Hebrews, because of its hall of fame of faith in chapter 11. I read from the beginning, though. Chapter 2 starts out, "We must pay the most careful attention, therefore, to what we have heard, so that we do not drift away." I'd done it again. Drifted. There He was, the secure log in the fast-moving rapids, and I forgot to hang on. I had to get back and hang on tight. I literally threw myself on the floor and bawled out my confession and a plea for forgiveness. Again.

I exercised the disciplines of Bible study and prayer that had become somewhat flabby. I grew to love and respect the sweet ladies that spent time with mom. Carol Darling was kind enough to spend some evenings or even nights with mom and dad so that Keith and I could visit Renée or do whatever else we needed to do. She and mom became fast friends, for which I'm truly grateful. Carol remains one of my closest friends. God's blessed her with the gift of encouragement—and those people are always in high demand.

So, mom's boldness, which I earlier shrank from, emboldened my faith anew. This series of events also crystallized mom's faith— she was baptized on October 16, 2001, in our pool. Keith baptized her. The two elders that first came to visit us looked on. Still gives me goosebumps. Does that date ring a bell? It should—your parents got married on that day a few years later. Both new beginnings. Mom knew Jesus long before that, so hers was more a re-commitment ceremony. She was eighty-one.

With my faith thus emboldened, I sought another way to serve. The Sunday school program had changed to an unfamiliar style, and with grown kids, I didn't see myself in that ministry anymore. Where God would lead me next, I never would have imagined in a million years.

"I have taken an oath and confirmed it, that I will follow your righteous laws." Psalm 119:106

CHAPTER ELEVEN

VERVE

"WE WANT TO RECLAIM THE ARTS FOR GOD." THAT'S what hooked me. J. K. and Elaine introduced a new drama ministry during a Sunday service at Metro. I'd just completed a thesis entitled, "Integrating the Arts in the Elementary Classroom." I picked up the "more information" they provided and went to the orientation the next week. When J. K. said that our unlikely group of drama wannabes should be the most expressive people in the church, the exit sign called my name. I was sure God wanted me there, but I sure didn't know why.

J. K. and Elaine, through their own gifted creativity and varied array of talents, turned our motley crew into a band on a mission. J. K. had us fast and pray to take this commitment seriously. He gave us a mission verse and a song. The verse is in the introduction to this memoir, Joshua 20:9. The song still stirs my soul, and if you've read this far, you'll understand. Here's the chorus of "Light the Fire in My Heart Again"[14]:

Light the fire (echo)
In my soul ((in my weary soul)
Fan the flame (echo)
Make me whole (make my spirit whole)
LORD You know (echo)
Where I've been (echo)
So light the fire
In my heart again.

He named us "Verve" - fiery passion, energy; symbolized by a flame.

To break our inhibitions, J. K. had us do decidedly un-adult things—like sashay backwards across the room or laugh like hyenas...things you're taught not to do in kindergarten! Like a drama boot camp, we trained to abandon individual propriety for team creativity.

The church sent us to a ZOE Conference in Tennessee—a national Christian conference for ministry leaders. The keynote message fanned a flame in my soul. Mike Cope, a well-known minister and professor, spoke of the freedom to physically express what we KNOW by faith. I mean, we move to secular music, but in church, we often praise God as if He's given us BAD news! Behind Mike as he spoke, married artists Jack and Jill Maxwell painted on a large mural. When they finished, there David danced unashamedly before the ark of God as he brought it to Jerusalem. I thought about the concept in simple terms. "If you're happy and you know it, clap your hands." To raise your hands in praise—or as a plea for help—is a natural outgrowth of joy that's based on knowledge. My earlier thought that to emote in church evidenced a baseless faith was baseless! Years later, when the Maxwells came to Metro, I had an opportunity to tell Jill of the impact that mural made in my life. She and Jack both autographed the poster they'd made of it. It hangs in our study.

J. K. invited any of us so inclined to write a sketch for Verve. I tried some; he red-penned them and handed them back. I kept on, determined not to cower to a red utensil. I learned. He suggested I might write a full-length play from one of the sketches I wrote. J. K. wrote a full-length play that we staged in the fall. These plays carried no Christian teaching—just a way to invite the community in for a free theatre event and a chance to get to know us a little. After we staged his play, I told him that someday, I might do as he'd suggested. He said, "Next year."

I found myself saying, "OK, I will!" I walked out thinking, *What did I just do?!* I wonder if he had the same thought.

Some five months later, I gave J. K. my draft. He suggested general edits but allowed me the rewrite. Some six weeks later, he accepted my script and, as director, continued to improve it. Verve staged my play, *Not Far Enough,* in the fall of 2001. It seemed well-received by our mostly church community who had to love us unconditionally. They applauded politely and didn't throw tomatoes.

2002 was a tough year at home. After a steady decline, dad passed away peacefully on January 23rd. Mom was alone again. In the spring, I thought she and I might travel a bit, but she couldn't. Leg pain afflicted her, for which she couldn't find remedy.

In July, Keith, already diabetic, was diagnosed with CHF—Congestive Heart Failure—and cardiomyopathy—a weak heart muscle. The doctor wouldn't predict his future, so I searched the internet for a prognosis (doesn't everybody?). Scary. So was the adjustment to the new drugs, which replaced my husband with a zombie. Keith could no longer work. He had a good job, still with the state, as facility coordinator for the Orlando headquarters of FDOT and the Highway Patrol. I looked in the mirror. There was no option but for me to go to work, something I'd prayed I'd not have to do. I was scared, but I would woman up and do it with God's help.

After I'd changed my major a few times, I held a degree in Elementary Education. I applied for a teaching position, but the timing wasn't ideal. We'd booked a cruise on the Delta Queen riverboat, from St. Louis to St. Paul, for late September, a month and a half after the school year began. That was the one thing on mom's bucket list. Mom was still in pain but still wanted to go. Her cousin, also recently widowed, enjoyed the trip with us. We spent a few days with family in St. Paul. We didn't know those days would be mom's last with them.

Concurrent with the decline of Keith's health and his diagnosis, we in Verve worked on a re-production of *Overboard,* the play written by J. K. that we'd performed in 2000. Rehearsals, characterization, memorization, costume creation—all of that vied for my attention. We staged the play in early September.

Somewhere in there, a good friend from Verve offered me a job. Actually, his wife suggested it, but he overheard, so he didn't have much choice but to make it official. He worked in insurance, a subject I'd avoided, but he thought he could train me. I knew I'd be a twenty-four/seven kind of teacher, whereas this nine-to-five gig would allow me the necessary family time. That, and truth be told, with my life tossed into a centrifuge, it felt more stable to work with a supportive friend.

I showed up for work in early October. Over cappuccino, Paul started my Insurance 101 course. He drew on a napkin: "This is a house..." I had to learn quickly because the office was very busy. I soon felt overwhelmed and—in Keith's presence—whined to our Bible study group. Michelle O'Neal, in that group, sent me a card filled with love, support, and from her own experience, a thought that Keith's adjustment to our role reversal might be as difficult for him. I found her that Sunday, thanked her for her insight, and asked her to be a close friend. Fortunately, she agreed. People that speak truth in love—those are your true friends.

That fall, mom got worse. She'd feel good every other day, but on the days in between, she'd be in bed with a fever and chills— like clockwork. Neither her doctor nor others at two different hospitals could diagnose her. After a month at Shands, a renowned teaching hospital, only one option promised relief. Mom opted for that one—hospice care. With that support, she died at home on December 23rd, 2002, eleven months to the day after dad's death. Keith, my brother Chuck, and I were with her at the end. That Christmas season was bittersweet. The reality of "God with us" spoke palpably to our gut-wrenched hearts, making it one of our most meaningful Christmases.

I think it was late 2002 that J. K. and Elaine left Verve and our church. Their faith took a different path. Verve's creative genius, energy, and talent—exited stage left. You know how God worked in the Bible with the likes of Gideon, Moses, and others who weren't natural leaders? Here too, I guess, He stripped away our human leadership so we'd have to depend on His. While I still dealt with the year's emotions, three of us initially took up the mantle of leadership. That gets messy, so Paul, my boss, accepted the leadership role in 2003. In an effort to ramp up our drama knowledge and skill, the church sent him and me to a drama conference in Kansas. The next year, two others joined us for a return trip. Several of us also attended acting classes at the local Shakespeare theater. As we learned to direct, we practiced on our team members. There are still a few scarred actors out there as a result.

When the time came to produce our now-annual play, we needed a director for the script we bought. Paul was "older" (my age) and thus perfect for the lead role. The rest of us were needed in supporting roles. Enter Brigitte Hill, the drama director of a nearby church. I'd crossed paths earlier with her on a drama blog. Keith and I were impressed by an Easter production she'd directed at her church. We also saw her act at the Theater Downtown in Orlando. She was a professional actor, so it took nerve to ask her to direct our play. To my surprise, she accepted—a fact for which many of us will be forever grateful.

After our play, Verve and Brigitte's drama team collaborated on a Christmas program that we did for both churches. She continued to work with us, and eventually, Brigitte and her husband, Jerry, placed membership at Metro. I'd like to think it was due to my constant nagging. A German, quick-witted, petite redhead who loved God and theatre, she'd serve Metro for years to come. Jerry wasn't just her plus one—he did sound and light and created any prop that Brigitte could envision—and she could envision some doozies.

My favorite collaboration with Brigitte was to write five-minute sketches for Dan Holland's sermons. Honestly, Dan didn't need dramatic help to communicate a message, but this was our passion. The plays, Christmas programs, and sundry other events all had their mission, but we felt this our most significant work. We'd start out with his message, pray about it, start to dramatize the heart of it, continue to write, and then look back at it to say, "Where'd that come from?" It's that sight of God's participation in the midst of a creative effort that not only builds faith but fires the passion to continue. And then to God be the glory.

That doesn't mean Dan used everything we wrote—that would have required us to read his mind, and we were never that fortunate. Brigitte and I would work separately sometimes or more often together through email, for days, finally email a script to Dan, and hold our breath. His responses were always concise: "Let's use this," or "Let's pass on this." If the former, we'd do an end-zone dance for a few minutes before we planned production. If the latter, we'd sigh, put our helmets back on, and line up for the next series.

I learned so much from Brigitte. Not just how to write, act, or direct, but how to truly live by faith. Her relationship with God was REAL. You would expect a professional actor to press for excellence and be firm with an actor who was late for rehearsal, but it took me aback when she took GOD to task. One night after a rehearsal for the Christmas program, we were alone in the church building. We lacked props she badly wanted. She looked slightly upward and spoke firmly, "God, this is Your play and if You want it done right, I need those rugs and I need them soon, or this play— Your play—isn't going on!" I stepped away from her just to be safe. Her rugs appeared within the week from an unexpected source. God was her partner, and she was straight with Him. I loved her for that more than anything.

J. K. personified Verve. Brigitte personified Verve. I can't thank God enough for the privilege to work with both. There are so many other people and events in Verve that challenged the wallflower in me to break free, but that would be another book.

Lucy, when God calls you out of your comfort zone, go. He'll be there. You'll make mistakes and learn. You'll have successes and grow in confidence. You'll find your passion. Most of all, you'll learn there's nothing that you and God can't handle.

As you'll see next, I needed that lesson for some off-stage drama too.

"My heart is set on keeping your decrees to the very end." Psalm 119:112

Chapter Twelve

FEED IT AND IT WILL GROW

"DO YOU HAVE TO GUARD YOUR HEART?" MICHELLE questioned me over coffee as my talk of work and Verve often raised Paul's name. My heart had been so wracked by grief and fear, I hadn't given much thought to its security. I knew down deep that I'd become emotionally dependent on Paul but rationalized it. "We're just friends; he's my boss, and we're co-workers in a ministry." He and I spent too much time together in legitimate pursuits—we solved insurance problems by day and Verve problems by night. I didn't mean to lean on him; he was just there all the time—a supportive Christian friend. Again, any time I drew nearer to God, Satan tried to counter.

For his own reasons, Paul participated less and less in Verve and then, after a few years, left our insurance agency to start his own with his son, Doug, who'd also worked with us. That was 2006. I knew the separation at work was necessary, but I won't lie— it made my drive to work very painful. Without work or Verve in common, I used any Sunday morning opportunity to start a conversation.

I sought counseling—not for this, but for a lifelong food addiction. The counselor's specialty was marriage and family therapy, so like a beachcomber with a metal detector, he unearthed my secret. His diagnosis? I couldn't accept how much God loves and values me. Why would he say that? Emotional dependency is when you expect someone else to fill some emptiness that only God can fill. You give another the responsibility for your self-worth and well-being. Guilty. My assignments were to 1) make and constantly review a list of twenty things I liked about myself (you have no idea how hard that was!), 2) avoid Paul completely (I had to ask his cooperation, to which he agreed), and 3) invest more in Keith. I learned that the partner most likely to leave a marriage is the one that has invested the least in it. I had no plan to leave my marriage, but ...ouch.

I actioned all three assignments. Keith's birthday was coming up, so I took the day off and treated him to a day at the Harley dealer with dinner at Ruth's Chris steak house. (That meal was so rich, I had to take a sick day the next day.) We launched a routine to meet for lunch once a week. I started praying every morning, not just for Keith's health, but for me to focus on his wonderful, God-given qualities and to adjust my attitude when pride reared its head. I heard once on the radio, "Gratitude helps you to see what's there, instead of what isn't." Lucy, I have to tell you this real change in my perspective transformed our marriage completely and for good. Did Keith change? No, he remains the same—has always loved me with a pure and patient heart. I've just decided to treat him as God would have me treat him, no matter my mood—even if he never replaces another toilet paper roll.

This change sounds easier than it felt. I knew what I had to do, and God gave me the strength to do it, but it was how Dan Holland described counseling—it's like physical therapy where you have to bend a body part in a way it hurts to go, to get it functional again (paraphrase). A song I mentioned before gave me fortitude: Hillsong's "This Is How We Overcome" (ibid). I often accuse Christian lyrics of torturous repetition, but this time, I needed that phrase a dozen times. In April of 2007, I wrote in my journal—to God: "Why do You love me? I doubt You, question You...but when I look back at what You've done in my life.... SHOW OFF!! And now this: yanking me back from drowning myself in a whirlpool, walking quietly behind me as I toddled down the barren path, looking for my lost friend...when I sadly realized the spell-binding image was hollow, You picked me up and brought me home."

God reminded me that you can't get so comfortable in your marriage or walk with God that you lose focus. You have to feed it—endlessly. If it doesn't grow, it stagnates. Nourishment must be intentional and planned, like you feed yourself. If you don't plan ahead but instead rely on junk food...well, you know what happens—blocked arteries of communication, shortness of patience, a weakened heart.

About seven years later, with my heart whole, wholly one with Keith and guarded by God with high walls, locked gates, cameras, alarms, and water cannons, I went to work with Paul and Doug's agency. It was Doug who then held the reins of their daily operations. Doug and I had run into each other regularly at a monthly networking group and vied for the same business. On many occasions, he asked me to join their now well-established team. I respected Doug. I knew he'd worked hard and learned all he could, to run the business. So, when I grew uncomfortable with a certain boss-employee relationship at our old agency (ironic, right?), I reached out to Doug. His was a mission-minded Christian agency, and many of his team had been discovered at his church. Keith was a full partner in this decision, and we agree it was a good one.

Paul's heart had always been in African missions, and he now spent a good part of his time there. Was it weird when Paul *was* in the office? Maybe initially, just due to remembered conviction, but after that I can honestly say no. I think we'd both been challenged by the other and, with God's help, learned. We conversed as friends, but any history on my part was just that.

My co-workers made the agency a challenging and enviable place to work—they were fun, young, professional, and hardworking. As experienced as I was in insurance, there were those on the new team that eclipsed me in knowledge, initiative, and speed (you know who you are). This was new, so I confided in my friend Michelle, who headed HR for a large company. She labeled me a "Steady Betty." I grew to be okay with that. I know my personality—I'm a good support person. I continued to do my best to earn my keep every day. Ultimately, I worked for God and saw my job as a ministry, to meet needs and solve problems. I hired a pragmatic cheerleader in the form of a mousepad with the words of Henry Ford: "Whether you think you can or think you can't, you're right." The position served me well until I retired in August 2019. My work friends were by and large a generation younger than me, but I miss them. It was thanks to them that I watched the thirty Marvel movies in a month, to understand the daily debates about Iron Man and Captain America. My trainee, Sarah, rewarded that effort with the Thor bobblehead who guards my desk and reminds me to stay in the fight.

And what of Verve? When Dan Holland left Metro, it started a "What happens now?" process for most of us in the congregation. As edifying as the new pastor tried to be, Brigitte and I watched Sunday morning drama get the hook. Keith and I stayed at Metro for a while, then felt the need to look elsewhere. Trent, the "new guy," couldn't stay long at Metro for many of the same reasons Dan left. Both Dan and Trent started church plants. We were torn. Do we go with Dan, whose lessons had so challenged us? Do we hear more of Trent's thoughts on God's Word? On what basis do we choose where to worship? On some weekends, we went to both services. Finally, after much prayer, we placed membership with Trent's group. When his church plant ran out of funds not even a year later, he moved back to Arizona about the same time Dan launched a new campus for "Real Life"—a mega-church in then eight locations. We checked it out, loved it immediately, and are still there. We've served at three different campuses and still think we're there by Design. With His hand in events, I'll never again dare to predict our future. (As I finish this memoir, I see Him calling me to a new mission, working with a church "community hub" in our neighborhood, to be held at a coffee shop where all proceeds go to end human trafficking).

Lucy, as I write this, you're about to become a teenager. The best advice I can offer is to settle in to God's embrace and let Him lead. When I was a teenager, I was sure I would be a nurse—like my mom. If you had told me that I'd drop out of the U of MN to marry a sailor, live all over the country, two years in Italy, go back to school for Educational Psychology, change my major to Spanish, then to Spanish/French Education, then to Elementary Education and then work in insurance for seventeen years, I'd have thought you were high on LSD (Google it). The only constant has been God—even when I doubted Him. Circumstances change, but He doesn't. He has been my strength, my rock, and refuge. It edifies my faith to look back and remember how far He's brought me. It's humbling to admit to you my foibles and struggles that the Nama in me would rather conceal, but if I can spare you and Lukas any of the pain I've caused myself, my humiliation will be well worth it.

God knows how quickly we forget. "Do this in remembrance of Me," He said (Luke 22:19). Years back, I had a near-death experience that helps me visualize how weak I am without Him. On a Good Friday, an undetected bleeding ulcer landed me in the ER with a hemoglobin count of 5.5. That's dangerously low. By the time the doctor rushed in to exclaim, "You have no blood in your body!" I was too weak to care. It took five units of blood over the weekend before I felt like me. Now, every time I look at the communion cup, I remember. It's only through Jesus's blood—His death and resurrection—that I have the ability and power to live the abundant life that only He can give.

And it IS abundant! It may not be materially lavish, but it's like having a bottomless well from which you can confidently fill your bucket with meaningful answers to your daily challenges. The abundant life flows into our marriage and through us to others. It's from that well that Keith and I draw the blessing of a home that is filled with the joy that passes all understanding. Every day. Does that mean an end to difficulty? No. Everyone has their own set of challenges, and we have ours. Keith's insulin pump has more accessories than do I and is more demanding. His cardiomyopathy requires an ICD/pacemaker to keep him in rhythm and give him a beat if he stops. He's regularly screened for a return of esophageal cancer. His faith has to battle depression from these chronic conditions and PTSD. He has submarine nightmares and wakes up fighting the air. Some days, he just goes back to bed. Those days are hard for me because I don't know how to help. So, I go to the well and find comfort, love, strength, patience, and trust.

And we are so grateful—that God has given us today, to get up and walk together, serve together as we can, watch a movie together, and be right where we are. For some unfathomable reason, Keith still professes and acts like he would rather be with me than anyone else, and I pray each day to be worthy of his love and that I'll generously express the love that I share for him. It's all possible because of God's love for us. Life isn't a Hallmark movie. Marriage takes work—and for us, God's work.

When you were a week old, Lucy, I held you in my arms, carried you around your parents' home, and sang, "You are my sunshine, my only sunshine." Same with Lukas after he was born. You two remain that sunshine—we light up when you're around—or on a video chat. We could not love you more, and because of that, I couldn't help but want so much for you to know the Secret of my life's joy. To borrow lyrics that resonate to both the navy wife and the "Verve" in me, He is the "King of my heart, the wind in my sails, my anchor in the waves, and the fire in my veins."[15]

My prayer for all of us echoes a song from the musical "Godspell": that we might see Him more clearly, love Him more dearly, follow Him more nearly, day by day.[16] Napa and I know that you and Lukas know Him, by the love and sweetness you always show. You have verve—His enthusiasm, energy, passion. How will you use it? I can't wait to see.

"Your word is a lamp for my feet, a light on my path."
Psalm 119:105

TRAVELOGUE

WE THOUGHT HIS TIME WAS SHORT, SO KEITH AND I took one last big trip in 2003, for three weeks. We saw *Les Mis* in London; sailed from the white cliffs of Dover; watched a "military tattoo" at the Edinburgh castle; learned about thatched roofs in the pristine beauty of the Faroe Islands; marveled at the production of geothermal energy in Reykjavik; hiked in Newfoundland, Nova Scotia, and Bar Harbor; and then toured NYC, where we saw the remnants of the 9/11 tragedy.

He was still alive in 2013, so we took one last big trip to cruise Australia's east coast and New Zealand. We sat at Sydney's Opera House, sipped cappuccino, and looked out over Sydney's bustling harbor at the Sydney Harbor Bridge. We hiked in Blue Mountain National Park and had tea on a Victorian-decorated tram as we toured Melbourne. We sailed the fjords of New Zealand's southern island on an unusually clear day. The rich, grassy green islands in the shimmering blue water made for the most beautiful landscape I'd ever seen. We got lost in Christchurch and almost missed our bus back to the ship.

Keith was still in good enough health to accompany me on two work trips to Birmingham, England. After the trade shows, we took the train to London. We toured Buckingham Palace in 2016, Queen Elizabeth's ninetieth year. Her most historic dresses were on display, with the "why" and "where" she wore each. We walked reverently through a history of notables at Westminster Abbey, toured the Royal Observatory and the Cutty Sark, and cruised the Thames. We walked in the steps of our tennis heroes at Wimbledon's All England Tennis and Croquet Club. We were at Windsor Castle long before Harry and Meghan married there. Our yeoman warder at the Tower of London regaled us with tales of its history and showed off the crown jewels.

Keith's kidneys didn't look good in 2017, so we took one last big trip. We'd planned to go with friends, but they couldn't go, so we took the trip they'd planned. It started in Belgium, where we spent three days. In Ypres, we witnessed the Armistice Day ceremony, where world leaders laid wreaths at the Menin Gate to commemorate the lives lost in WWI. We toured Flanders Field museum and saw the grave of John McCrae, who wrote the poem "In Flanders Field" that we'd heard at the Veterans' Day ceremony here in Sanford. After those three days, it was a sixteen-day river cruise, to which we added three days in Paris, on our own. We toured the WWII museum in Nuremberg and saw the site of the infamous trials. We toured cathedral after cathedral, overwhelmed with their opulence and sheer size. We learned of the real challenges of maintaining those architectural masterpieces.

That reminds me of Notre Dame in Paris. Before the awful fire, I climbed the south tower with Flat Lucy and Flat Lukas in my pocket, so you can say you did it too. I have pictures to prove it, should anyone ask.

By 2019, Keith had been diagnosed with esophageal cancer, so we took one last big trip—to Paris, London, and Ireland. It was actually his plan for my retirement gift, and I almost talked him out of it. Glad I didn't. He'd planned it so we'd tour the Palace of Versailles on our anniversary, forty-one years after we celebrated our fifth anniversary at King Ludwig's replica of Versailles in Bavaria. That fifth anniversary was the most romantic setting we've ever enjoyed: Ludwig's palace is on an island in Lake Chiemsee—a ferry takes you to it. We toured the palace in the afternoon. That evening, we awaited our turn to enter the palace again for a concert of Mozart's music by a string quartet. It was dark in the formal gardens, where we sat on a concrete bench, with the candle-lit palace in the distance. Nearby were softly-lit fountains that provided their own gentle rhythm to the faint streams of music that could be heard from the first performance of the evening. Centered over the palace was a reddish moon; we found out later it was an eclipse. Horse-drawn carriages delivered passengers from the ferry to the palace entrance. The clip-clop of hooves lent a Jane Austen feel to the evening. The concert itself, in the palace, was almost anti-climactic. Even Hallmark can't set such a scene.

The fact that Keith not only remembered the date of that fifth anniversary night, but planned the excursion to the REAL Versailles on our forty-sixth anniversary, impressed me even more than did the lavish palace and its endless grounds with fountains that danced to classical music.

On that same 2019 trip, we toured the Palais Garnier in Paris, which inspired *The Phantom of the Opera.* We travelled by

Chunnel to see *Phantom* performed at Her Majesty's Theatre in London. We took the train through Wales, ferried to Dublin, and spent a week exploring the island's perimeter. In Belfast, we felt the tension of the separated Protestant and Catholic communities. On the north and west coasts, the Giant's Causeway and Cliffs of Moher reminded us of the majesty, diversity, and creativity of The Architect who is our God.

In addition to these adventures, we've cruised the Caribbean and part of Alaska's coastline with friends. For Renée's college graduation gift, we took her to visit Jake, then stationed in Hawaii. There, we all toured Oahu, Maui, and Kauai.

St. Augustine said, "The world is a book and those who don't travel read only one page."[17] Compared to other travelers, we've only read a couple of chapters. These are just a few of our experiences, but every one makes us want to explore that much more.

These were all to be our "last trips"—we'd never have travelled this much if we didn't think it somewhat urgent to do so. Elisabeth Kübler-Ross, in her classic book, *On Death and Dying,*[18] said, "It's only when we truly know and understand that we have a limited time on earth—and that we have no way of knowing when our time is up—that we will begin to live each day to the fullest, as if it was the only one we had." I had friends that thought me kind of morbid as I spoke of Keith's future in finite terms, and they were right. But considering what it led to, I have no regrets. Life is short—for all of us—and Napa and I hope that—whether through mission trips or just to sightsee—you take opportunity to explore God's world.

I don't know if we have any "last big trips" in our future, but even if not, we have the memories. Currently, we have an unusually beautiful place to enjoy them, here on the river. The best part of any journey—geographical or through life, is the people you meet along the way. I've mentioned a few already. Here, at the river, are more friends who've travelled life journeys that inspire me. Melanie Perschka, a close longtime friend who lives downstream from us, is an overcomer, and I pray she writes a memoir while I can still read. Then there's my Riverwalk friends, who gather at Sherry and Felix's coffee shop downstairs: Jana first, a ministry leader and organic, creative, disciplined life explorer, whose core is love. Then Jim, who's ten years my senior and still bikes one hundred miles a week. He carried my backpack, shared his water, and coached me up a mountain after I fell and bruised a rib on the Appalachian Trail. His wife, Pat, a dulcimer virtuoso, is the reason I'm going to hit Keith up for a keyboard after I finish writing this memoir. David raises orchids and honeybees, teaches at his church, and— like Jim—will do anything he can for anybody in need. Amy is a super-mom, co-leader of a global ministry with her husband, and connects women for mutual encouragement. Of course, there are others—so many that have inspired me, I can't begin to list them. I haven't even started on people at church that have had major influence. There are two who don't fit either of the above categories but must be mentioned, and those are Carolyn and Martin. Once neighbors way back in the day, we've celebrated many life events and holidays together. They've been there for us many times. Our best friend is Jesus, without Whom all is meaningless, a chasing after wind. The only journey that truly matters is the one with Him, and we pray that your adventures on the planet will bring you the same joy as we've found with Him and His people.

We are so rich in memories and friendships, I feel almost guilty. Far more blessings than I deserve. Lucy, you and Lukas rank at the very top of our "blessings" list, and I pray that the sight of God's presence in my life will help you see the possibilities for yours. Napa and I are so honored to be your grandparents, and we love you both very, very, very much.

Hugs and Kisses from us both,
Nama

ABOUT THE AUTHOR

KATHY LONGTIN IS A CHRISTIAN, PROUD WIFE OF A retired naval submariner, proud mom of Jacob and Renée, and proud grandmother, aka "Nama" of Lucy and Lukas. She taught Sunday school for many years and has written and co-written dozens of contemporary sketches for her church, plus a full-length play for the community. Kathy and her husband, Keith, serve with their local church in central Florida, however they hear God's direction to do so.

ENDNOTES

1   C. S. Lewis, Chronicles of Narnia, Geoffrey Bles, The Bodley Head (HarperCollins, 1950-1956).

2   Elevation Worship, "See A Victory," recorded 2019, track #3 on At Midnight, Sony/ATV Music Publishing LLC.

3   "On His Blindness," John Milton, 1655.

4   "USS Pintado (SSN 672)" Wikipedia, ed. January 2010.

5   "Phrases and Philosophies for the Use of the Young, via Oscar Wilde's Wit & Wisdom" (Dover Publications, Inc, 1998).

6   Francis Schaeffer, How Should We Then Live? The Rise and Decline of Western Thought and Culture (Wheaton, IL: Crossway Books, 1976).

7   Lawrence O. Richards and Gary J. Bredfeldt, Creative Bible Teaching (1998). Lawrence O. Richards, A Theology of Children's Ministry (1983).

8   Andersen, Fairy Tales Told for Children (Copenhagen: C.A. Reitzel, April 7, 1837).

[9]   Peter Billingsley, A Christmas Story, directed by Bob Clark (1983; Beverly Hills: MGM/UA Entertainment Co.), TBS.

[10]   Jane Austen, Persuasion (London: John Murray, 1818).

[11]   Rick Warren, The Purpose-Driven Life, 1st Edition (Zondervan, October 8, 2002).

[12]   Hillsong Worship, "This Is How We Overcome," recorded 1998, Hillsong Music Publishing, Admin. by Capitol CMG Publishing.

[13]   Pride and Prejudice, BBC, 1995.

[14]   Bill Maxwell, recorded 1987, Bloodsmith Music.

[15]   Taken from "King of My Heart" by Sarah and John Mark McMillan, recorded 2015, Jesus Culture Music, under exclusive license to Sparrow Records.

[16]   Stephen Schwartz, "Day by Day," recorded 1971. Words originally attributed to a prayer by Richard, Bishop of Chichester, translated to English and published in Songs of Praise, Enlarged Edition (1931).

[17]   Commonly attributed to St. Augustine of Hippo, but as quoted in "Select Proverbs of All Nations" by "Thomas Fielding" (John Wade), 1824, p. 216, (via wikiquote).

[18]   On Death and Dying (New York: The Macmillan Company, 1969).

CPSIA information can be obtained
at www.ICGtesting.com
Printed in the USA
LVHW042007261020
669857LV00016B/2216